# The Family Debt Reset

# The Family Debt Reset

*Pay Off the Plastic, Reclaim Your Peace,
and Take Back Your Financial Future*

Anthony C. Lumpkin

ACL Publishing, LLC

The Family Debt Reset: Pay Off the Plastic, Reclaim Your Peace, and Take Back Your Financial Future

This book is intended for general informational purposes only and does not constitute professional financial, legal, or tax advice. The author and publisher are not responsible for any actions taken based on the information in this book. Readers should consult a qualified professional for advice specific to their financial situation.

Names and identifying details in this book have been changed to protect the privacy of individuals.

ISBN: 978-1-7371443-8-0 (Paperback)

First Edition

Printed in the United States of America

# Dedication

*To every family sitting at the kitchen table
tonight wondering if things can change. They
can. This book is the proof you asked for.*

# Contents

# Appendix: The Family Debt Reset Toolkit

# Why This Book Matters Now and How the 90-Day Reset Works

You already know you have a problem. You don't need another book to tell you that.

You know it when your phone buzzes with a payment reminder and you swipe it away without looking. You know it when you do the math on the minimum payments and realize you'll be paying off a dinner you ate three years ago for another six years. You know it at 11:30 at night when the house is quiet and you open the banking app just to see if the number changed, even though you know it didn't.

You don't need to be convinced that credit card debt is a problem. You need someone to show you a way through it that actually works for a household like yours.

That's what this book is.

## Why Most Debt Advice Doesn't Stick

There's no shortage of money advice out there. Podcasts, YouTube videos, apps, spreadsheets, gurus with six-figure courses. And some of it is fine. Some of it is even smart. But most of it is built for a person who lives alone, has one income stream, and makes decisions without checking with anybody else.

That's not your life.

Your life has a partner who handles money differently than you do. Or kids who need things this week that weren't in the budget. Or a car that breaks down on Tuesday and a dental bill that shows up on Thursday. Your life has a refrigerator that needs to be full by Sunday and a rent check that clears whether you're ready or not.

Most debt advice ignores all of that. It gives you a formula and assumes you'll follow it. It tells you to stop spending without asking what your household actually needs to survive this month.

It treats debt like a math problem when really it's a family problem. An emotional problem. A trust problem. A problem that sits between two people at the kitchen table and makes everything feel harder than it should.

That's why this book is different. Not because the math is revolutionary. It's not. The snowball method and the avalanche method have been around for decades. What's different is that this book was built for the way families actually live. Messy schedules. Tight months. Real arguments. Real setbacks. Real people who want to do better but keep hitting walls they didn't see coming.

* * *

## Shame Didn't Get You Into This. It Won't Get You Out.

Let me say something up front. You are not in debt because you're bad with money.

You might be in debt because childcare costs more than a mortgage in some cities. Because health insurance deductibles are brutal. Because someone in your house got sick and the bills came faster than the paychecks. Because you grew up without anybody teaching you how credit works, and by the time you figured it out, you were already carrying a balance.

Or maybe you just made choices. Normal choices. A couch when the old one broke. Back-to-school clothes. A weekend trip because your family needed a break and you put it on the card because the money wasn't there yet.

None of that makes you irresponsible. It makes you human. And it makes you the same as tens of millions of other households in this country who are carrying credit card debt and feeling alone in it.

This book will never talk down to you. It won't lecture you. It won't tell you to stop buying coffee like that's the reason you're $18,000 in the hole. What it will do is meet you where you are, give you something practical to do about it, and respect you enough to tell the truth while it does.

* * *

# The 90-Day Family Debt Reset

This book is built around one core idea: in 90 days, you can change the direction of your family's financial life. Not fix everything. Not be debt-free by day 91. But fundamentally shift how your household handles money, talks about money, and attacks the debt that's been sitting on your shoulders.

Ninety days. Three months. Three phases.

**Phase 1: Face It.** Month one. This is where you stop guessing and start knowing. You look at every balance, every interest rate, every minimum payment. You build a snapshot of where your family actually stands—not where you hope you stand or where you were six months ago. Then you stop the bleeding. You freeze new debt. You set emergency rules. You create a short-term plan to hold the line while you build the real strategy.

**Phase 2: Fix It.** Month two. This is where you go on offense. You choose a payoff plan that fits your household. You find hidden money in your existing spending. You explore ways to bring in extra income. And you learn how to talk about all of it with your partner without it turning into a fight. That last part matters more than most people think.

**Phase 3: Future-Proof It.** Month three. This is where you protect what you've built. You create family money rules that actually stick. You prepare for setbacks so they don't send you backwards. You build your first safety nets. And you start to imagine what life looks like on the other side of this—not just surviving, but choosing.

Each phase has chapters that walk you through every step. Nothing is theoretical. Everything is built for a real family with a real budget and real stress.

* * *

## How to Use This Book

Read it in order. The chapters build on each other. Skipping ahead to the payoff plan before you've done the honest numbers work in Phase 1 is like painting a wall before you've patched the holes. It looks productive, but it doesn't hold.

If you're doing this with a partner, read it together when you can. Some couples read a chapter a week and talk about it during their money check-in. Others read separately and compare notes. There's no wrong way as long as both of you are engaged. And if your partner isn't ready to engage yet, that's okay. Chapter 7 is written specifically for that situation.

If you're doing this alone—single parent, sole earner, or just the only one in your household willing to look at the numbers right now—this book still works. The framework is the same. The steps are the same. You just won't have a partner to split the emotional weight with, which means the chapters on mindset, setbacks, and vision matter even more for you.

Every chapter ends with a section called "This Week's Reset." That's your action step. Something small, practical, and specific you can do before you move to the next chapter. Don't skip those. They're where the real change happens—not in the reading, but in the doing.

* * *

## What This Book Won't Do

It won't promise you'll be debt-free in 90 days. Some of you are carrying $8,000. Some of you are carrying $45,000. The timeline depends on your numbers. What 90 days will give you is a system, a rhythm, and momentum. That's what most families are missing. Not willpower. A structure that fits their life.

It also won't replace professional help if you need it. If you're facing bankruptcy, a lawsuit from a creditor, or a financial situation that feels legally complicated, talk to a professional. This book is a practical guide, not legal or financial counsel.

What it will do is give you something most debt books don't. A way to work through this as a family. Not just a budget plan—a reset for how your household thinks about, talks about, and deals with money. That's the part nobody else is writing about. And that's the part that makes the math actually work.

* * *

## One Last Thing Before You Start

You picked up this book because something needs to change. Maybe you're tired of the stress. Maybe you had a conversation that didn't go well. Maybe you just looked at a balance and thought, this can't keep going.

Whatever brought you here, you're in the right place. Not because this book has magic answers. Because you're ready to do something about it, and that's the only thing that actually matters.

Let's get started. Phase 1 begins now.

**PHASE 1: FACE IT**
*Month 1*

### CHAPTER 1

# How Your Family Got Here and What It's Really Costing You

Nobody wakes up one morning $23,000 in credit card debt.

It doesn't happen like that. There's no single afternoon where you sit down and decide to bury your family in interest payments. No moment where both of you agree, yes, let's trade our peace of mind for a 24.99% APR. It doesn't work that way.

It works like this.

The furnace dies in January. You don't have $3,200 in savings, because who does. So you put it on the Visa. You'll pay it off in a few months. Except then the car needs tires in March. And the kids need school supplies in August. And somebody's tooth cracks in October and the insurance only covers half.

Each time, it's the same math. We need this now. We don't have the cash now. The card is right there.

And each time, you tell yourself you'll catch up. But catching up never quite happens, because life doesn't pause while you pay things down. It just keeps billing you.

That's how most families get here. Not through recklessness. Through the ordinary cost of staying alive.

* * *

## The Debt Didn't Start With One Bad Choice

I want to be clear about something early, because the rest of this book depends on it: you didn't do this to yourself. At least not the way you think you did.

Yes, you swiped the card. Nobody forced you. But the system around you made it almost impossible not to. Credit card companies don't make money on people who pay their balance in full every month. They make money on people who carry a balance. That's you. That's their business model. And they are very, very good at it.

They sent you the card when you turned eighteen. They raised your limit without you asking. They offered zero-percent balance transfers that quietly reset to 22% after twelve months. They designed the minimum payment

to be small enough that it feels manageable—
and just large enough that you never actually
get ahead.

On top of that, you're living in an economy
where wages haven't kept up with the cost of
housing, food, childcare, or healthcare. The gap
between what your household earns and what it
costs to run a household has been getting wider
for years. Credit cards fill that gap. Not because
people are irresponsible. Because the math
doesn't work without them.

So when you look at your total balance and feel
a wave of shame, I want you to understand what
you're really looking at. You're looking at a
stack of real needs that came at the wrong time.
You're looking at a system that was built to
keep you in debt. And you're looking at the
price of trying to hold a family together in a
world that doesn't make that easy.

That doesn't mean you're off the hook. You still
have to fix it. But fixing it starts with
understanding how you got here—honestly,
without the guilt trip.

## The Slow Slide Nobody Notices

Emergency spending is the obvious door into debt. Everybody understands that. But there's a quieter door that most families walk through without realizing it.

Lifestyle creep.

It works like this. You get a raise—maybe an extra $400 a month after taxes. You don't sit down and say, "Let's spend all of this." What happens is smaller. You upgrade the streaming package. You start ordering groceries instead of going to the store because it saves time. The kids get signed up for one more activity. You eat out on Fridays because you've earned it. You switch to a nicer phone plan.

None of those feel like mistakes. Each one feels reasonable on its own. But together, they eat the raise. And then some.

A couple I talked to—we'll call them Derek and Aisha—made a combined $92,000 a year. Not struggling. Not rich. Solid middle ground. But they were carrying $19,000 in credit card debt and couldn't figure out where the money was going. When they finally sat down and added it all up—subscriptions, memberships, delivery fees, convenience charges, the little upgrades they'd made over three years—it came to almost $1,100 a month in spending that didn't exist when they were making $20,000 less.

They weren't living extravagantly. They'd just drifted. Each small decision made sense at the time. But the total didn't.

That's the thing about lifestyle creep. It's invisible until you add it up. And by the time you notice, you've been subsidizing the gap with plastic.

* * *

## Why Minimum Payments Keep You Stuck

The minimum payment is one of the most effective traps in consumer finance. And it works because it feels like progress.

You owe $8,000 on a card with a 23% interest rate. Your minimum payment is $160 a month. You pay it on time. Every month. You're responsible. You're doing what they asked.

At that rate, it will take you just over nine years to pay it off. And you'll pay roughly $9,400 in interest alone. Meaning you'll hand the credit card company more in interest than you originally spent.

Read that again. More in interest than you spent.

And that's on one card. Most families are carrying three to five. Multiply that math across all of them, and you start to see why minimum payments don't feel like progress. They are progress—just barely. Like walking on a treadmill and wondering why you're not getting anywhere.

The minimum payment was designed to keep you in the game as long as possible. Not to help you win. The credit card company doesn't want you to default, because then they lose money. But they also don't want you to pay it off, because then they stop making money. The minimum is the sweet spot—for them. You stay current. They collect interest. Everybody's happy except you.

Understanding this doesn't fix it yet. That comes in Phase 2 when you pick your payoff plan. But knowing what the minimum payment actually does—and who it's designed to benefit—is the first step in deciding to do something different.

* * *

## What Debt Actually Costs Your Family

The credit card statement shows you the financial cost. It doesn't show you the rest.

It doesn't show the argument that started because one person saw a charge the other didn't mention. It doesn't show the parent who skipped their own doctor's appointment because the copay would've been one more thing on the card. It doesn't show the kid who asked to sign up for basketball and watched their mom hesitate for just a second too long before saying yes.

Debt takes things you can't put a number on.

It takes sleep. You're up at midnight running numbers in your head, trying to figure out which bill to pay first. You do the math three different ways and none of them work. You put the phone down, stare at the ceiling, and wait for the alarm.

It takes presence. You're at your kid's school event, but you're not really there. You're thinking about the payment that's due Friday and whether the check will clear before the auto-pay hits.

It takes trust. Small lies start forming. "How much was that?" "Oh, it was on sale." Not because you're dishonest. Because the truth is heavy and you're tired of carrying it into every conversation.

It takes options. You stay at a job you hate because you can't afford the gap between paychecks. You turn down a family trip because you know what it would do to the balance. You stop dreaming about the house, the move, the retirement account, because all of that feels like a fantasy when you're still paying off last year's groceries.

And maybe the worst part—it takes your belief that things can change. After enough months of making payments that barely move the needle, you start to accept it. This is just how it is. We're a family that carries debt. That becomes the story, and once it does, it's harder to write a new one.

I'm telling you right now: that story is wrong. You are not stuck. You're uninformed about your options, under-supported in your plan, and exhausted from doing it alone. All three of those things are fixable. That's what the next eleven chapters are for.

* * *

## You're Not Broken. You Need a Reset.

Here is where you are right now. You're at the beginning of Phase 1 of the 90-Day Family Debt Reset. This phase is called Face It. And this chapter—the one you just read—is the hardest part of it.

Not because the information is complicated. Because it asks you to look at your situation honestly, without the usual shields. No pretending the balance is lower than it is. No telling yourself it'll just work out. No blaming your partner or your job or the economy—even though all of those might be real factors.

Facing it just means saying: this is where we are. Not where we want to be. Not where we should be. Where we are.

And here's the thing about that moment. It feels awful. But it's the same moment every family who's ever paid off serious debt has gone through. The ones who made it didn't have more money than you. They didn't have more discipline. They just got to this moment—the honest one—and decided to keep going instead of looking away.

You're at that moment right now.

Next chapter, we're going to get specific. You'll pull out every card, every balance, every rate, every minimum payment. You'll build your Family Debt Snapshot. That's your starting line. And once you have it, everything that follows in this book will make more sense, because you'll finally be making decisions based on real numbers instead of guesses.

But for tonight, just sit with this: you understand how you got here. And it wasn't because something is wrong with you. It was because life is expensive, the system isn't built in your favor, and nobody handed you a plan.

Now you have one.

* * *

## This Week's Reset

Before you move to Chapter 2, do these three things.

**One.** Gather every credit card statement you have. Physical or digital. If you've been avoiding opening them, this is the week you open them. You don't have to do anything with them yet. Just have them in one place.

**Two.** Write down the total number of credit cards your household is carrying right now. Not the balances—just how many cards. That single number is more revealing than you think.

**Three.** Have one honest conversation. With your partner, with yourself, or even just a sentence written in the margin of this page. Answer this: what is this debt costing my family beyond money?

That's it. You're not solving anything yet. You're just turning the lights on in the room you've been avoiding.

Phase 1 is called Face It for a reason. You just did the hardest part.



## CHAPTER 2

# Face It. Know Your Real Numbers.

Ask someone how much credit card debt they're carrying and watch what happens. Their eyes move. They look up or to the side. They say something like "a few thousand" or "more than I'd like."

They don't say a number.

Not because they're lying. Because they honestly don't know. Or they knew three months ago and haven't looked since. Or they know the number on one card but not the other three. Or they know the total but they've never added the interest rates together, so the number they carry in their head is a balance that stopped being accurate the day after they checked it.

This is how most families live with debt. In the blur. Close enough to know it's bad. Far enough from the details to avoid feeling the full weight of it.

That ends today.

Not because I want to make you uncomfortable. Because you cannot fix a problem you haven't measured. Every chapter after this one depends on you knowing your real numbers. Not the rounded version. Not the best guess. The actual, honest, all-cards-on-the-table numbers that your household is carrying right now.

* * *

## No More Guessing

There's a reason you've been guessing. Guessing hurts less.

When you don't know the exact number, you can negotiate with yourself. You can tell yourself it's probably around twelve thousand, which feels manageable. You can avoid logging into the Capital One app because if you don't see the balance, it isn't real yet. You can keep the number soft and blurry so it doesn't sit in your chest all day.

I get it. That's a survival instinct. When the truth feels like too much, we protect ourselves by staying a few inches away from it.

But here's what happens when you guess. You make decisions based on a number that doesn't exist. You allocate money toward a balance that's actually higher. You skip a payment on the card you think is fine, not realizing the interest pushed it past the limit. You build a plan around a financial picture that's out of focus, and then you wonder why the plan doesn't hold.

A woman I spoke to—let's call her Nicole—told me she spent two years "paying extra" on her credit cards. She was proud of it. She'd round up every month, throw an extra fifty or hundred at the balance whenever she could. But she never looked at the interest. Her main card was at 27.49%. The extra payments she was making weren't even covering the interest that accrued between statements. For two years, she was walking uphill on a belt that moved faster than her feet.

She didn't find out until she finally logged in and saw the balance was higher than when she started. She sat in her car in the driveway and cried. Not because the number was impossible. Because she'd been doing the right thing—or what felt like the right thing—and nobody told her the math was working against her the whole time.

That's what guessing costs. Not just confusion. Lost time. Lost money. And lost faith in your own effort.

The 90-Day Family Debt Reset starts with the truth. All of it. In one place. That's what you're going to build in this chapter.

* * *

## Build Your Family Debt Snapshot

This is the most important exercise in the entire book. Not because it's complicated. Because everything else is built on top of it.

Here's what you're going to do. Get a piece of paper, open a spreadsheet, or use the Debt Tracker in the appendix. Whatever format works for you. The tool doesn't matter. The honesty does.

For every credit card your household carries, write down five things.

**The name of the card.** Visa, Mastercard, store card, whatever it is. If you've got a Target card with a balance from two Christmases ago, it goes on the list. If there's a card in a drawer you haven't used in months but still carries a balance, it goes on the list. Every single one.

**The current balance.** Not what you remember. The real number. Log in. Look at it. Write it down. If you're doing this with a partner, do it together. No card gets left out because it's embarrassing.

**The interest rate (APR).** This is the number most families never look at. It's on your statement, usually on the first or last page in small print. If you have different rates for purchases and cash advances, write down both. The APR is the engine that drives your debt forward while you sleep. You need to see it.

**The minimum payment.** What's the smallest amount they'll accept this month without charging you a late fee or reporting you? That's your floor. Right now, most families are paying at or near this number. We're going to change that, but first you need to know what it is.

**The due date.** Write it down for every card. One of the most common ways families fall behind isn't that they can't afford the payment. It's that they missed the date. Late fees stack. Your rate can increase. Your credit score takes a hit. Knowing when every payment is due is basic, boring, and critical.

When you're done, you should be looking at a complete picture of your credit card debt. Every card. Every balance. Every rate. Every minimum. Every due date. This is your Family Debt Snapshot.

Sit with it for a minute. The number might be bigger than you thought. That's okay. Knowing is better than guessing. It has to be, because guessing is what got you stuck.

* * *

## What Your Interest Rate Is Really Doing

Most people know their interest rate is "high." Very few understand what it actually does to their money month after month.

Let me make it concrete.

Say you're carrying $6,000 on a card with a 24% APR. That rate isn't annual the way you'd expect—it gets divided by twelve and charged monthly. So every month, the credit card company adds roughly $120 in interest to your balance. Before you've bought a single thing. Before you've swiped the card once. Just for owing the money.

Now look at your minimum payment on that card. It's probably around $140 to $160. Subtract the $120 in interest, and you're paying down maybe $20 to $40 of actual debt each month. On a $6,000 balance. At that pace, you're looking at more than a decade to pay it off—and you'll pay nearly as much in interest as you originally owed.

That's one card. Do that math across three or four, and you start to see the hole.

I'm not telling you this to scare you. I'm telling you because the interest rate determines which card you should attack first, how much your extra payments actually matter, and whether a balance transfer or negotiation might save you real money. When you get to Chapter 4 and choose your payoff plan, the interest rate is one of the two most important numbers on the page. If you don't know it now, you'll be guessing then. And we just talked about what guessing costs.

* * *

## The Number Most Families Avoid

You've written down every card. You've got balances, rates, minimums, and due dates. Now comes the part most families skip.

Add it up.

Total it. Every card. One number.

This is the number people avoid. Not the individual balances—those feel manageable in isolation. Three thousand here. Five thousand there. A couple thousand on the store card. Each one sits in its own corner and stays tolerable. But when you add them together, the weight of the full picture hits different.

Maybe it's $14,000. Maybe it's $28,000. Maybe it's $41,000. Whatever it is, your first instinct will be to explain it away. That includes the medical bills. Some of that is from the move. Half of it is old. Your brain will try to soften the number because the raw total feels like a verdict.

It's not a verdict. It's a starting line.

Derek and Aisha from Chapter 1—the couple with $19,000 in debt on a $92,000 income—told me that adding up the total was the worst and best thing they did. Worst because the number was bigger than either of them expected. Aisha had been carrying a store card balance she hadn't mentioned. Derek had a cash advance from eight months earlier he thought he'd paid off. When they saw the real total for the first time, sitting together at their kitchen table with a calculator and four statements between them, Aisha said she felt sick.

Then something unexpected happened. The tension dropped. Not immediately. But within a few days. Because the worst part wasn't the number. The worst part was not knowing. Once they had it, they could stop imagining and start planning. The anxiety didn't vanish, but it got quieter. It went from a constant low hum to something with an edge they could push back against.

That's what the total does. It replaces dread with data. And data you can work with.

* * *

## Know What's Coming In and Going Out

Your debt snapshot tells you what you owe. Now you need to see what your household actually works with every month.

This part is less dramatic than the debt total, but it matters just as much. Because the gap between what comes in and what goes out is the space where your debt either grows or shrinks. Right now, for most families reading this, that gap is either razor-thin or nonexistent. That's why the cards keep getting used.

Start with income. What hits your bank account every month after taxes? Not gross pay—net. The amount you actually see. If you have irregular income—freelance work, tips, seasonal hours—use the average of your last three months. Don't use your best month. Use the realistic one.

Then write down your fixed monthly obligations. Rent or mortgage. Car payment. Insurance. Utilities. Phone. Internet. Childcare. Student loans if you have them. These are the non-negotiable ones—the things that get paid every single month no matter what else happens.

After that, estimate your variable spending. Groceries. Gas. Household supplies. Haircuts. School lunches. The stuff that changes month to month but never goes to zero. Don't estimate from memory—pull up your bank statement and debit card transactions for the last thirty days and add it up. Most people are surprised. The grocery number is almost always higher than they think. And the miscellaneous spending—pharmacy runs, a grab at the drive-through, the birthday gift you picked up last minute, the thing you tossed in the cart because it was on sale—that category alone can eat $300 to $500 a month without leaving a single memorable purchase behind.

A guy I worked with—let's call him Ray—was convinced his family spent about $600 a month on groceries. He said it with confidence. When his wife pulled the actual transactions for the last four weeks, the number was $1,040. He stared at the screen for a long time. It wasn't that they were buying expensive food. It was the frequency. Four or five trips a week instead of one or two planned ones. Each trip added things that weren't on any list. Snacks. Drinks. Whatever looked good near the register. None of it felt like a problem in the moment. Added up, it was a $400 gap between what he believed and what was real.

That's the kind of thing this exercise exposes. Not bad behavior. Blind spots.

Now subtract. Income minus fixed expenses minus variable spending. Whatever's left is what you have to work with. For some of you, that number is a few hundred dollars. For others, it's barely anything. And for some of you, the math goes negative, which means you're covering the gap with credit cards every single month and the hole is getting deeper while you tread water. If that's you, don't panic. That's exactly what Chapter 3 and Chapter 5 are designed to fix.

The point of this exercise isn't to make a budget. Not yet. The point is to see the full picture for the first time. You know what you owe. Now you know what you have. Those two numbers together are the foundation for every decision you'll make from here forward.

* * *

## Your Starting Line Starts Here

You now have something most families in debt don't have. Clarity.

You know every card. You know every balance, every rate, every minimum payment, every due date. You know your total. You know your monthly income and where it goes. That's more financial awareness than some households develop in years of making payments.

This doesn't feel like a win. I know. Staring at the full picture of your debt isn't the kind of thing that makes you want to celebrate. But it is the most important thing you've done in this process so far—because from this point on, every decision you make will be based on reality. Not hope. Not avoidance. Not a rough number you came up with in the shower.

If you're doing this with a partner, something might have shifted between you already. Maybe you argued a little while you were adding things up. Maybe one of you went quiet. Or maybe— and this happens more often than people expect —the conversation was easier than you thought it would be. Because the hard part was never the numbers. It was agreeing to look at them in the same room, at the same time, without flinching.

You might be thinking the number is too big. That there's no way your household can pay this off on what you earn. I hear you. But I also need you to trust the process for a few more chapters. In Phase 2, you're going to find money you didn't know you had. You're going to learn how to bring in extra income. You're going to pick a payoff plan that fits your family, not a textbook family. All of that is coming.

That all starts with this. The snapshot. The real numbers. The starting line.

You're standing on it right now. Next chapter, we're going to stop the bleeding.

* * *

## This Week's Reset

**One.** Build your Family Debt Snapshot. Every card. Balance, interest rate, minimum payment, due date. Use the Debt Tracker in the appendix or any format that works. Do it today, not tomorrow. Tomorrow turns into next week.

**Two.** Add up the total. Write it down somewhere you'll see it. Not to punish yourself. To anchor yourself. That number is your starting line, and you need to remember what it was so you can watch it change.

**Three.** Calculate your monthly income minus fixed expenses minus variable spending. If the number is positive, that's your current debt-fighting margin—however small. If it's negative, mark it. That tells you exactly where to focus in the next two chapters.

**Four.** If you have a partner, do this together. Sit down. Show each other. No judgment, no lectures. Just the numbers on the table. If your partner isn't ready, do it yourself and keep the snapshot somewhere safe. You may need it for both of you later.

You don't need to make a plan yet. You don't need to call the credit card company. You don't need to cut anything up or close any accounts. All you need right now is the truth, in writing, in one place.

That's your reset for the week. And it's more progress than most families make in a year.



## CHAPTER 3

# Freeze It. Stop the Bleeding.

There's a moment in every emergency room visit where the doctors stop trying to diagnose the problem and just focus on one thing: stop the bleeding. Doesn't matter what caused the injury. Doesn't matter what the long-term treatment plan looks like. None of that helps if the patient is still losing blood.

Your debt works the same way.

You've done the hard part. You looked at your numbers. You built the snapshot. You know what you owe, what it's costing you, and where your money goes every month. That took courage, and I don't say that lightly.

But right now, while you're reading this, the debt is still growing. Every swipe, every auto-charge, every "just this once" is adding to the balance you just stared down. The interest doesn't pause because you're working on a plan. The minimum payments don't shrink because you're more aware. The hole is still getting deeper.

Before we talk about payoff strategies or finding hidden money or earning extra income—before any of that—we have to stop making it worse.

That's what this chapter is. The tourniquet.

* * *

## You Can't Outrun New Debt

This is the part nobody wants to hear.

You can't pay off credit card debt while you're still adding to it. Not effectively. Not in any way that creates real momentum. You'll feel busy. You'll feel like you're making progress. But the balance won't move.

I know why the cards keep coming out. I'm not going to pretend it's simple. The gas tank is empty on Wednesday and payday isn't until Friday. The kid needs medicine and you don't have $30 in the checking account. The dishwasher breaks and you can't leave standing water in the kitchen for two weeks while you figure it out. Real things. Things that can't wait.

But mixed in with those real emergencies are the quiet swipes that don't feel like choices anymore. Groceries on the card because it's easier. The subscription you forgot to cancel. Lunch out because you didn't pack one and you're tired. Thirty-eight dollars at Amazon for something you needed—or thought you needed—at eleven o'clock at night.

Every one of those charges feeds the balance. And every one of them makes your eventual payoff harder, longer, and more expensive. The interest on today's swipe starts accruing tomorrow. In a month, that $38 impulse buy has already cost you $39. In a year, it's closer to $47. And it keeps growing until you pay it in full.

Freezing your credit card use doesn't mean you're failing. It means you're finally treating the problem with the seriousness it requires. A doctor wouldn't keep operating while the patient is bleeding out. You can't build a payoff plan while the debt is still accumulating.

First, we stop the bleeding. Then we operate.

* * *

## The Emergency Rule Every Family Needs

I'm about to tell you to stop using your credit cards. And your first reaction is going to be: what if something happens?

That's fair. Because something always happens.

This is where most debt books lose people. They say "cut up the cards" like it's that easy. Like you don't live in a world where the car can break down tomorrow, the urgent care visit costs $200, and your kid needs new shoes before Monday. Telling a family under financial pressure to just stop using credit is like telling someone underwater to just breathe normally. The advice isn't wrong. It's just disconnected from reality.

So instead of a hard rule that breaks the first time life hits, here's a rule that bends without breaking.

**The card is for emergencies only. And you define the emergency in advance.**

Right now, before anything goes wrong, sit down and write a short list of what counts as a genuine emergency. Not a loose definition. Specific situations. Here's a starting point.

**Yes, it's an emergency:** Car repair that affects your ability to get to work. Medical expense that can't wait. Home repair that creates a safety risk. Essential childcare cost with no alternative.

**No, it's not an emergency:** A sale that ends tonight. Takeout because you don't feel like cooking. A convenience purchase because cash feels tight this week. Something your kid wants but doesn't need before Friday.

Write your version of this list. Put it on the fridge, in your wallet, or in the notes app on your phone. The goal isn't perfection. The goal is that when the moment comes—and it will—you don't have to make the decision under pressure. The decision is already made. You just follow the rule.

A couple I know—Terrence and Val—kept a folded index card in the kitchen drawer next to the credit card. Three lines. "Is someone's safety at risk? Can this wait 48 hours? Can we cover it with what's in checking?" If the answer was no, yes, or yes, the card stayed in the drawer. That card saved them from at least four unnecessary charges in the first two weeks alone. Not because they were undisciplined. Because having the rule in writing removed the argument. Neither one had to be the bad guy. The card was the bad guy.



## How to Create a Spending Freeze Without Panic

A spending freeze sounds extreme. It's not. It's a temporary reset. Thirty days. That's all you're committing to right now.

During those thirty days, you only spend on four categories: housing, transportation, food from the grocery store, and true emergencies as defined by your list. Everything else pauses. Not forever. For one month.

That means no new clothes unless something is literally falling apart. No subscriptions you forgot you had—cancel them this week or pause them. No eating out. No Amazon at midnight. No "treating yourself" because the week was hard. The week is always hard. That's not a reason. That's a pattern.

I know how this sounds. Like deprivation. Like punishment. It's not. A spending freeze is triage. You're redirecting every available dollar toward stabilizing your household instead of scattering it across things that feel necessary in the moment but don't move the needle.

Here's what makes it work.

**Tell your household.** A freeze only works when everyone knows it's happening. If you go silent and just start saying no to everything, your partner and your kids will feel blindsided. Have the conversation. Keep it short. "We're going to try something for thirty days. We're going to cut way back on spending so we can get a handle on our debt. It's not permanent. It's a reset." That's enough.

**Remove the easy swipes.** Take the credit card off your Amazon account. Remove it from your phone's digital wallet. Unsubscribe from the retail emails that hit your inbox every morning with flash sales designed to make you click. You don't need willpower if you remove the trigger. If the card isn't saved in the app, there's a pause between the impulse and the purchase. That pause is where your money stays in your pocket.

**Plan your meals.** Food is the biggest variable expense most families have, and it's the easiest one to overspend on without realizing it. Pick five dinners for the week. Buy what you need. Cook at home. It doesn't have to be fancy. It has to be intentional. The $12 you save skipping the drive-through on Tuesday adds up to over $350 in a year. And that's just one day a week.

**Give each person a small allowance.** This is important. A freeze that allows zero personal spending creates resentment. Give each adult in the household $20 to $30 for the week, cash, to spend on whatever they want. Coffee, a snack, a magazine, whatever. When it's gone, it's gone. But having something—even a little—makes the restriction feel human instead of suffocating.

Val told me later that the weekly cash allowance was the thing that kept Terrence in. He didn't care about the budget. He didn't care about the spreadsheet. But the $25 in his wallet every Monday made him feel like he still had some control over his own life. That mattered more than any debt strategy she could have shown him.

$$* * *$$

## What to Do If You Still Need the Cards to Survive

Some of you read the last two sections and felt a knot in your stomach. Not because you disagree. Because right now, today, the credit card is the only thing between your family and going without.

If your monthly income doesn't cover your monthly expenses—if the math from Chapter 2 went negative—then telling you to freeze the cards without addressing the gap would be irresponsible. I'm not going to do that.

Here's what I want you to do instead.

First, separate the essential card spending from the non-essential. If you're putting groceries on the card because there's no cash, that's survival. If you're also putting DoorDash on the card because it's Tuesday and nobody wants to cook, that's habit. The first one might be unavoidable right now. The second one isn't. Start by cutting the second category completely, even if the first one stays for a few more weeks.

Second, track every card charge this month. Every one. Write it down or screenshot it. At the end of thirty days, sort them into two columns: had to and chose to. Most families find that 30 to 40 percent of their card spending falls into the "chose to" column. That's the money you're going to recover.

Third, know that this is temporary. The income chapter is coming. The money leak audit is coming. The payoff plan is coming. If you're in a position where the cards are keeping the lights on, you're not behind in this book. You're exactly where this chapter expects some readers to be. The 90-Day Family Debt Reset doesn't pretend that everyone starts from the same place. It just asks you to start from an honest one.

The goal right now isn't to go cold turkey. It's to go conscious. Every time you reach for the card, ask yourself: is this the emergency list or is this the habit? That single question, asked consistently, will slow the bleeding even if it doesn't stop it overnight.

* * *

## Your First Small Win

Something happens in the first week of a spending freeze that nobody talks about.

You feel in control.

Maybe not right away. The first two or three days are annoying. You reach for your phone to order something and remember you can't. You drive past the coffee shop and keep going. You open the Amazon app out of habit, see the empty cart, and close it. Each of those moments has a small sting to it.

But by day four or five, something shifts. You start to notice the money sitting still. The checking account balance at the end of the day is the same as it was that morning. Nothing leaked out. You look at your card statement and there's no new activity. Just silence. And that silence feels different than you expected. It doesn't feel like deprivation. It feels like traction.

A woman named Sharice—single mom, two boys, working full time as a medical biller—told me about her first freeze. She was skeptical. She said she'd tried cutting back before and it never lasted because she'd feel guilty buying her kids a $3 bag of chips at the gas station. But this time, she set the emergency rules, gave herself and each kid a $10 weekly cash allowance, and committed to thirty days.

On day nine, her oldest asked for pizza money for a school event. She almost reached for the card. Then she remembered the $10 she'd set aside for him. He used that. She didn't swipe. And when she checked her balance that night, she realized she'd gone nine days without a single credit card charge. She said it was the first time in two years she could remember that happening.

Nine days. No charges. For Sharice, that was the first proof in two years that she could do this. It doesn't show up on a spreadsheet. Nobody gives you a trophy. But it rewires something in your brain. It proves you can operate without the card being your safety net for every small moment. And once you believe that, the bigger changes in Phase 2 start to feel possible.

Small wins build confidence. Confidence builds consistency. Consistency is what actually pays off debt. The spending freeze isn't the strategy. It's the foundation the strategy needs to stand on.

* * *

## The Bleeding Has Stopped. Now What?

You're at the end of Phase 1.

Three chapters ago, your debt was a blur—scattered across apps and envelopes and conversations you didn't finish. Now you have a snapshot with real numbers, a household budget with honest math, and a freeze in place between your family and new debt. You faced it. On paper, with rules your household can follow.

Phase 2 starts in the next chapter, and the energy shifts. You're done defending. Now you go on offense. You're going to pick a payoff strategy that matches your family. You're going to find money hiding in your current spending. You're going to explore real ways to bring in extra income this month. And you're going to learn how to talk about all of it with your partner without the conversation falling apart.

Phase 1 was about honesty. Phase 2 is about momentum.

Let's build it.

* * *

## This Week's Reset

**One.** Write your household emergency rule. Define what counts as a genuine emergency and what doesn't. Put it somewhere visible—the fridge, the kitchen drawer, your phone. Make it a rule both partners agree on, not one person's decision.

**Two.** Remove your credit card from every digital wallet, saved payment method, and

online store account. All of them. If the card
number is memorized, that makes this harder—
but removing the one-click access matters more
than you think.

**Three.** Start your thirty-day spending freeze.
Only spend on housing, transportation,
groceries, and emergencies from your list. Give
each adult a small weekly cash allowance so the
freeze feels sustainable.

**Four.** If you're still relying on the card for
essential spending, track every charge this
week. Write it down. At the end of seven days,
sort each charge into "had to" or "chose to."
That split is your first real diagnostic.

**Five.** Tell someone what you're doing. Your
partner, a friend, a family member. Not for
accountability in the guilt sense. Because saying
it out loud makes it real. And once it's real, it's
harder to quietly let it go.

Phase 1 is complete. You faced it. You froze it.
Now it's time to fix it.

## PHASE 2: FIX IT
*Month 2*

## CHAPTER 4

# Fix It. Choose Your Debt Payoff Plan.

Carlos kept a sticky note on his bathroom mirror for four months. It said $26,814. That was his family's total credit card debt across five cards—the number he'd written down the night he and his wife Janelle finally built their debt snapshot.

He stared at it every morning while he brushed his teeth. Some days it motivated him. Most days it just made him tired. Because knowing the number wasn't the same as knowing what to do about it.

He'd Googled "how to pay off credit card debt" at least a dozen times. Every article said the same two things: snowball or avalanche. But nobody explained which one was actually right for a household that was already stretched thin, with different cards at different rates, and a partner who panicked any time the budget got mentioned.

If that sounds familiar, this chapter is where you stop reading about debt payoff strategies and actually pick one.

* * *

## There Is No Perfect Plan. Only the One You'll Follow.

Let's get this out of the way early. The internet will argue about debt payoff strategies until the end of time. Snowball people think avalanche people are ignoring psychology. Avalanche people think snowball people are wasting money on interest. Both sides have spreadsheets. Both sides have math. Both sides are right—about the math.

But math isn't why most people fail at paying off debt.

People fail because the plan doesn't fit their life. They pick the "optimal" strategy, follow it for six weeks, hit a rough month, and abandon it. Not because the strategy was wrong. Because it was built for a spreadsheet, not a household with three kids and a $400 car repair on the second Tuesday of the month.

The best debt payoff plan is the one you'll actually stick with when things get hard. When the fridge breaks. When someone gets sick. When you're four months in and the balance still feels enormous. The plan that survives those months is the one that works. Everything else is theory.

I'm going to show you three approaches. You're going to pick one. Not the "best" one. The one that fits your family, your temperament, and your situation. Then you're going to commit to it for at least ninety days before you second-guess it.

* * *

## The Snowball Method

The snowball method says: forget the interest rates. Line up your debts from smallest balance to largest. Pay the minimum on everything except the smallest one. Throw every extra dollar you have at that smallest card until it's gone. Then take everything you were paying on that card—the minimum plus the extra—and roll it into the next smallest. Keep going until they're all gone.

Here's what that looks like in real numbers. Say you have four cards. A $640 store card, a $2,100 Visa, a $5,800 Mastercard, and a $9,200 Discover. Your total minimums across all four are about $380. On top of that, you've found $200 a month in extra money from your spending freeze and your money leak audit. In the snowball, that entire $200 goes at the $640 card. In about three months, it's gone. Now you take the $200 plus the $25 minimum you were paying on the store card—$225—and slam it into the Visa on top of its minimum. The payments get bigger as each card falls.

The math doesn't love this approach. If your smallest card has a 14% rate and your biggest card has a 27% rate, you're technically letting the most expensive debt grow while you clean up the cheap stuff. A financial advisor would wince.

But here's what the math doesn't account for: the feeling of paying something off completely.

When that first card hits zero—when you log in and see $0.00 where there used to be $1,200—something changes in your chest. Not your finances. Your belief. You did it. One card. Gone. And for a lot of families, that feeling is the fuel that makes the second card possible, and the third, and the fourth.

Janelle—Carlos's wife—was a snowball person and didn't know it. She needed to see progress. She needed a win she could point to when things felt hopeless. Their smallest card was a $640 store card from a furniture purchase. They knocked it out in seven weeks. She told Carlos that was the night she finally believed they could do this. Not because of the amount. Because something was finished.

**Best for:** Families who need early motivation. People who get discouraged easily. Households where one or both partners need to see visible progress to stay committed.

* * *

## The Avalanche Method

The avalanche method says: line up your debts from highest interest rate to lowest. Pay the minimum on everything except the card with the highest rate. Attack that one first. When it's gone, move to the next highest. Repeat.

This approach saves you the most money. Period. Because you're eliminating the debt that's costing you the most per month first. Every dollar you put toward a 27% card is working harder than a dollar you put toward a 14% card. On a $5,800 balance at 27%, you're losing about $130 a month just to interest. At 14%, that same balance costs you about $68. The avalanche attacks the $130 drain first, which means more of your money goes toward actual debt reduction from day one.

Over time—especially if your total debt is above $15,000—the avalanche can save you hundreds or even thousands in interest compared to the snowball. For a family carrying $26,000 across five cards with rates ranging from 15% to 27%, the difference can be over $2,000 in saved interest. That's real money. Groceries for months. A starter emergency fund. It matters.

The problem is time. The highest-rate card might also be your biggest balance. Which means you could be grinding for months before you see a card hit zero. And months of effort without a visible finish line can break a family's motivation. You're doing the right thing. You're saving money. But it doesn't feel like it.

Carlos was an avalanche thinker. He'd pull up the interest calculations and show Janelle how much they were losing every month to the 24.99% Visa. He was right. But she didn't want to hear about theoretical savings. She wanted to see a card disappear. This became a real tension between them—not because either one was wrong, but because they were solving the same problem with different brains.

**Best for:** Families with large interest rate gaps between cards. People who are motivated by logic and long-term math. Households where the total debt is high enough that interest savings make a meaningful difference.

* * *

## The Hybrid Method

This is the one nobody talks about, and it's the one most real families end up using.

The hybrid method says: start with a quick snowball win to build momentum, then switch to the avalanche for the rest.

Look at your debt snapshot. Find the card with the smallest balance—something you can realistically pay off in four to eight weeks. Attack that first. Get the win. Feel it. Then take everything you were paying on that card and redirect it to the card with the highest interest rate. From there, you follow the avalanche.

You get the psychological win early. Then you get the mathematical advantage for the long haul. It's a compromise, and compromises sometimes lose a little efficiency—maybe a few hundred dollars in interest over the life of the payoff compared to a pure avalanche. But a plan that keeps both partners engaged and doesn't collapse after month two is worth more than theoretical savings you never actually collect.

The hybrid also works well when your debt snapshot has an obvious quick kill. If one card is under $800 and the rest are all above $3,000, knocking out that small card first barely costs you any interest and gives your household a concrete reason to keep going. You're not choosing emotion over math. You're using emotion to protect the math.

This is what Carlos and Janelle chose. They knocked out the $640 store card first—Janelle's win. Then they pivoted to the 24.99% Visa—Carlos's logic. By the time they hit the Visa, they already had proof that they could finish something. That made the long grind on the bigger card feel survivable.

**Best for:** Couples who think differently about money. Families who need a fast win but also carry high-interest debt. Anyone who's tried a payoff method before and quit.

* * *

## Choose Your Family Debt Attack Plan

Pull out your debt snapshot from Chapter 2. You need it open for this part.

Look at two things. First, how different are your interest rates? If your rates range from 18% to 26%, the avalanche advantage is real but moderate. If they range from 12% to 29%, the spread matters more and avalanche saves you significant money. If all your cards are within a few points of each other, the order barely matters—pick snowball and enjoy the wins.

Second, how much does your household need early motivation? Be honest. If you or your partner has a history of starting financial plans and quitting after a few weeks, the snowball or hybrid gives you something to hold onto early. If both of you are patient, analytical, and motivated by long-term outcome, the avalanche won't break you.

Here's a simple way to decide.

**Small rate spread, need motivation fast:** Snowball.

**Large rate spread, both partners are patient:** Avalanche.

**Mixed feelings, one partner needs wins and the other needs logic:** Hybrid.

**Not sure at all:** Start with the hybrid. It gives you the best of both and you can adjust later.

Once you choose, write it down. Not in your head. On the same page as your debt snapshot. Circle the card you're attacking first. That's your target. Every extra dollar this month goes there. Everything else gets the minimum.

And here's the rule that protects you: commit to your method for ninety days before you reconsider. Don't switch after three weeks because you read a Reddit thread that says avalanche is better. Don't switch because a coworker told you about some app that "optimizes everything." Switching strategies every month is worse than picking a mediocre one and sticking with it. Every time you restart, you lose momentum. You lose the mental rhythm. You go back to staring at the full balance instead of focusing on the target. Consistency beats optimization every single time.

Carlos and Janelle almost switched methods twice in the first six weeks. Both times, Carlos had found a new calculator online that showed them saving more money with a different approach. Both times, Janelle talked him off the ledge. "We already started. Let's just finish." She was right. The plan they stuck with wasn't the most efficient plan on paper. But it was the plan they actually followed. And that's the only plan that pays off a single dollar.

* * *

## How to Stay Consistent When the Balance Barely Moves

I'm going to tell you something nobody tells you in the payoff chapters of most books. There will be months where you do everything right—you follow the plan, you don't swipe the card, you throw extra money at the target—and the balance barely moves.

That's not failure. That's interest working against you in real time. And it's the exact moment most people quit.

You made a $300 extra payment and the balance only dropped $180 because $120 went to interest. You think: what's the point? The point is that without that payment, the balance would have gone up. You didn't just move forward. You stopped going backward. That shift doesn't feel like victory. It feels like running in place. But it's not. It's the moment the math starts turning in your favor, and you have to survive it to get to the good part.

The good part is when the snowball or avalanche effect kicks in. When the first card is gone and you roll that payment into the next one, the extra money hitting the target card gets bigger. That's when the balances start moving faster. That's when you log in and see a number that's noticeably different from last month. But you only get there if you push through the slow early months without abandoning the method.

Here's what helps during those months.

**Track the total, not just one card.** If you're focused on one card that's dropping slowly, pull back and look at the overall number across all cards. Sometimes the total is moving even when the target card feels stuck.

**Track how much you've paid, not just what's left.** Keep a running total of every dollar you've put toward debt since you started. That number only goes up. On a hard month, that's the number worth looking at.

**Revisit your debt snapshot monthly.** Update the balances. Compare them to where you started. Even a $400 drop across all cards in one month is real movement. Write the new total next to the old one. Let yourself see the gap.

Carlos taped a piece of graph paper to the inside of his closet door. Every month, he'd mark the new total debt number. The line went down slowly—painfully slowly some months. One month it barely moved at all because the car needed new brakes and they'd had to dip into money earmarked for the extra payment. But the next month the line dropped again. He said there were nights when he'd open the closet just to look at the line and remind himself the direction was right. Janelle thought it was obsessive. He thought it was survival. It was probably both. But that piece of paper cost nothing and kept him in the game for months when the statements alone would have broken him.

Find your version of the graph paper. Something physical. Something you can see without logging into an app. The app shows you the balance. The physical tracker shows you the trend. And the trend is what carries you.

*　*　*

## This Week's Reset

**One.** Open your debt snapshot. Sort your cards by balance (smallest to largest) and by interest rate (highest to lowest). Write both lists. Seeing your debt organized both ways will make the next step clearer.

**Two.** Choose your method. Snowball, avalanche, or hybrid. Don't overthink it. If you're stuck, start with the hybrid. Circle the first card you're attacking.

**Three.** Determine your extra payment amount. Look at the number from Chapter 2—your income minus expenses. Whatever margin you have, even $50, that's your monthly weapon against the target card. Everything else gets the minimum.

**Four.** If you have a partner, choose the method together. Talk through which approach fits how each of you thinks about money. If you can't agree, the hybrid is your compromise—it respects both perspectives.

**Five.** Start a tracking system. A spreadsheet, a notebook, a piece of graph paper in the closet. Whatever works. Write down today's total. This is the number you'll measure every month from here forward.

You have a plan now. Not a hope. Not a wish. A method with a target and a direction. Phase 2 is about offense, and you just made your first move.

PHASE 2: FIX IT
*Month 2*

# CHAPTER 5

# The Hidden $500. Money Your Family Is Already Losing.

Monique found $487 in one evening.

Not under the couch cushions. Not in a forgotten savings account. She found it in her own monthly spending—charges she'd been paying for months, some of them for over a year, without ever thinking about them.

A streaming service she'd signed up for during the pandemic and hadn't opened since the summer. A gym membership her husband stopped using in March. A cloud storage upgrade she didn't need because her phone plan already included it. An identity protection service she didn't remember authorizing. A meal kit subscription she'd paused twice but never actually canceled, and it had quietly reactivated both times.

Each charge was small. $9.99 here. $14.95 there. $49 for the gym. Nothing that screamed on a bank statement. Nothing that triggered an alert or a second look. But when she pulled up three months of transactions and highlighted every recurring charge she couldn't immediately justify, the total came to $487 a month.

That's $5,844 a year. Going nowhere.

Monique wasn't careless. She was busy. She was a working mom with two kids, a full-time job, and a household to run. The charges were small enough to ignore and automatic enough to forget. And that's exactly how they're designed to work.

* * *

## The Money Leak Audit

Your family is losing money right now. Not to some dramatic financial mistake. To the slow, quiet drip of charges you've stopped noticing.

This section is about finding that money. All of it. And once you find it, redirecting every recovered dollar into your debt payoff plan from Chapter 4. This isn't about earning more yet—

that's Chapter 6. This is about keeping the money you already have.

Here's how to run your Money Leak Audit. It takes about forty-five minutes. Do it with your partner if you can. Do it alone if you have to. But do it this week.

**Step one: Pull up three months of bank and credit card statements.** Not one month. Three. One month can hide things that only hit quarterly or every other billing cycle. Three months shows you the pattern. Use your banking app, download the PDFs, whatever is easiest. Just get them all in front of you.

**Step two: Highlight every recurring charge.** Subscriptions. Memberships. Auto-renewals. Monthly services. Insurance auto-drafts. Anything that charges you on a regular schedule without you actively choosing to pay it each time. Don't judge them yet. Just mark them.

**Step three: For each one, ask three questions.** Did I use this in the last thirty days? If I canceled today, would it affect my household this week? Would I sign up for this again right now at this price? If the answer to all three is no, it's a leak.

**Step four: Add up the leaks.** Write the total at the bottom of the page. That's your monthly recovery amount. That money is going to your target card from Chapter 4, starting immediately.

Most families find between $120 and $500 in leaks. Some find more. The number almost always surprises people—not because the individual charges are large, but because there are so many of them. They accumulate like dust. You don't see it building until someone makes you look.

* * *

## The Silent Budget Killers

Subscriptions are the obvious leaks. Most people expect to find a few of those. But there's a second category of spending that bleeds money just as fast, and it's harder to spot because it doesn't show up as a neat monthly charge. These are the silent budget killers—the habits and patterns that cost your household hundreds a month without ever appearing on a subscription list.

**Late fees.** The average late fee on a credit card is $32 to $41. Miss one payment on two cards, and that's $70 gone before you've bought a single thing. Over a year, a family that misses even one payment every other month is handing over $200 to $400 in fees alone. Set up auto-pay for the minimum on every card. Not because the minimum is your goal—it's not. Because it prevents a $35 penalty for something that takes thirty seconds to fix.

**Convenience charges and delivery fees.** Grocery delivery. DoorDash. Instacart tips and service fees. These aren't luxuries for some families—they're time trades. But the markup is real. A $60 grocery order can cost $78 by the time the delivery fee, service fee, and tip are added. Do that weekly and you're paying an extra $72 a month for the same food you could buy in the store. That's almost $900 a year.

During a debt reset, that's money your target card needs more than DoorDash does.

**Insurance you haven't reviewed.** Car insurance is the biggest one. Most families set it up, turn on auto-pay, and don't look at it for two or three years. In that time, rates change, discounts expire, and competitors drop their prices. A thirty-minute phone call or online comparison can save $40 to $100 a month. That's not an exaggeration—it's one of the most consistent savings most households can find. Same thing with renters insurance and phone protection plans. Review them once a year. Cancel what you don't need. Negotiate what you do.

**Your phone plan.** If you're on one of the big carriers paying $160 to $200 a month for two lines, look at the prepaid and MVNO options. Carriers like Mint Mobile, Visible, and Cricket run on the same networks for half the cost. Switching two lines could save you $60 to $80 a month. That alone is $720 to $960 a year—real money that changes your payoff timeline.

**Food waste.** This is the one nobody tracks and almost everybody is guilty of. The bag of spinach that turns to liquid in the back of the fridge. The leftovers nobody eats. The bananas that go brown by Wednesday. The average American household wastes roughly $1,500 worth of food a year. You won't recover all of that. But even cutting food waste in half—by planning meals, buying less per trip, and actually eating what's in the fridge before buying more—can save your family $50 to $75 a month.

**Bank fees you forgot about.** Overdraft fees. Monthly maintenance charges on a checking account that requires a minimum balance you haven't met in six months. ATM fees because you used the wrong machine in a hurry. Paper statement fees. These are small charges that banks count on you ignoring—and they add up to billions in revenue industry-wide every year. Check your last three statements. If you're paying a monthly maintenance fee, call your bank and ask how to get it waived, or switch to a free checking account. If you're getting hit with overdraft fees regularly, turn off overdraft protection and let the card decline. A declined card at the register is embarrassing for a second. A $35 overdraft fee is expensive for a month.

None of these categories look dangerous on their own. That's the problem. They're designed to be small enough that you don't fight them. But your household isn't dealing with one of them. You're dealing with six or seven at the same time, and the total is real money that could be attacking your debt every month instead of evaporating.

* * *

## How to Find Extra Cash This Week

The Money Leak Audit shows you monthly savings. But there's also immediate money sitting in your household right now that you can recover in the next seven days.

**Cancel first, think later.** For every subscription or service you flagged as a leak, cancel it today. Not next week. Today. Most of them take two minutes. Some will let you "pause" instead of cancel—don't pause. Cancel. If you miss it in a month, you can always re-subscribe. But pausing is how these services sneak back onto your statement.

**Call your credit card companies.** Ask for a lower interest rate. Say this: "I've been a customer for [X years]. I'm working on paying down my balance. Can you lower my APR?" It takes five minutes. Some will say no. Some will drop your rate by two to five points. On a $6,000 balance, dropping from 24% to 20% saves you about $20 a month in interest. It's not dramatic. But it's free money you get by asking a question.

**Check for unclaimed money.** Go to your state's unclaimed property website. Search your name. It takes thirty seconds. Old utility deposits, forgotten refunds, overpaid insurance premiums—millions of dollars sit unclaimed across the country because people don't know to look. You might find nothing. Or you might find $50 or $200 you didn't know existed.

**Review every auto-draft.** Go through your checking account and identify every automatic payment. Some of them are essential: rent, car payment, utilities. Others might be services you barely use or could temporarily pause. That app you downloaded for the kids three months ago that's been charging $7.99 a week—kill it.

A man named Greg did this audit on a Saturday morning while his wife took the kids to the park. Ninety minutes. He canceled four subscriptions, called his car insurance and saved $47 a month by switching to a higher deductible, and found $138 in unclaimed property from an old apartment deposit he'd forgotten about. Total monthly recovery: $114. One-time recovery: $138. He put the $138 directly toward his target card that afternoon. He said it felt like finding cash in a coat pocket—except it was real money that actually moved his balance.

* * *

## Why Small Fixes Add Up Fast

I know what you might be thinking. Forty-seven dollars on insurance. Twelve dollars on a subscription. Nine dollars on a streaming app.

That's not going to fix $22,000 in credit card debt.

You're right. Individually, none of those numbers change your life. But this chapter isn't about one fix. It's about all of them at once.

Let's run the math on a realistic recovery. Say your Money Leak Audit finds the following: two unused subscriptions at $12 and $15 a month, a gym membership at $49 nobody is using, a phone plan switch that saves $65 a month, reduced grocery delivery spending that saves $60 a month, and a successful insurance call that drops your premium by $47 a month. Total monthly recovery: $248.

Now watch what that does to your debt. You were making minimum payments on everything and throwing an extra $150 a month at your target card from the margin you found in Chapter 2. Add the $248 you just recovered. Your monthly debt weapon is now $398. On a card at 22% interest, that's the difference between paying it off in three and a half years and paying it off in about fourteen months.

Same income. Same job. Same household. You just stopped the leaks.

And here's the part that matters most for your family: you didn't sacrifice anything real. You didn't give up meals. You didn't take the kids out of activities. You didn't downgrade your life. You just stopped paying for things you weren't using and found cheaper versions of things you were. The quality of your daily life barely changes. The speed of your debt payoff changes dramatically.

That's why this chapter exists. Not because $12 matters. Because $12 times everything matters.

* * *

## What to Do With Every Dollar You Recover

This is the part most people get wrong. They find the extra money—and then it disappears.

Not into anything dramatic. It just... absorbs. The checking account has an extra $200 in it at the end of the month, and instead of sending it to the credit card, it gets spent on something else. Not a splurge. Just life. Groceries run a little high. Someone needs gas. A bill comes in a day early. The money dissolves into the month like it was never there.

Prevent that. Here's how.

**Move the recovered money immediately.** The day a subscription cancels and frees up $15 a month, set up an automatic extra payment to your target card for that amount. Don't let it sit in checking. Don't "plan to send it later." Automate it. The money should leave your account before you have a chance to think of another use for it.

**Stack your recoveries.** Every new dollar you free up gets added on top of the last one. Canceled the gym? That's $49. Switched phone plans? That's another $65. Each recovery stacks into a single, growing extra payment that hits your target card every month. Think of it as a debt snowball within the snowball—your extra payment amount keeps getting bigger as you find more leaks.

**Record every recovery.** Keep a running list of what you found and how much it saves you per month. Tape it next to your debt snapshot. Not just for tracking—for morale. When you're three months into this and feeling like the progress is slow, that list is proof that you're fighting with everything you've got. You didn't just wait for the debt to go away. You went looking for the money to kill it.

Monique—from the opening of this chapter—put her entire $487 recovery into her target card the month she found it. Her balance dropped by more in that single month than it had in the previous four months combined. She called her sister that night and said, "I can't believe how much money we were just giving away." Her sister ran the audit the next weekend and found $310.

That's how this works. You find the money. You redirect the money. And you do it fast enough that the money doesn't have time to vanish into the routine.

* * *

# This Week's Reset

**One.** Run your Money Leak Audit. Pull three months of bank and credit card statements. Highlight every recurring charge. Ask the three questions. Add up the total. Use the Money Leak Audit worksheet in the appendix or a blank sheet of paper. Forty-five minutes.

**Two.** Cancel every leak today. Not this weekend. Not when you get around to it. Open the apps, log into the websites, and cancel. If something requires a phone call, put it on your calendar for tomorrow at lunch.

**Three.** Call at least one credit card company and ask for a lower rate. Use the script in this chapter. It takes five minutes. The worst they can say is no.

**Four.** Search your state's unclaimed property website. Put any recovered money directly toward your target card.

**Five.** Set up automatic extra payments for every dollar you recovered. Don't let the savings sit in checking. Move them to the target card before the month absorbs them.

You didn't earn more money this week. You recovered money that was already yours. And now every dollar of it is working against your debt instead of disappearing into charges you didn't notice.

Next chapter, we talk about the other side of this equation—bringing in new money. Because finding the leaks is half the fix. The other half is making more than you spend.



CHAPTER 6

# Earn Your Way Out. Side Income Your Family Can Start This Month.

Andre was a forklift operator. Five days a week, ten-hour shifts, $21 an hour. After taxes, insurance, and his 401k contribution, he brought home about $2,900 a month. His wife Keisha worked part-time at a daycare so they could stagger childcare for their two boys. Together they made enough to cover the bills—

barely—but not enough to make a dent in the $17,400 they owed across four credit cards.

He'd done the Chapter 5 audit. Found $168 in monthly leaks. Canceled everything he could. But after the spending freeze and the leak recovery, his extra payment toward the target card was $215 a month. At that pace, full payoff was still over three years away. Three years of grinding. Three years of saying no. Three years of watching the balance crawl down while the interest kept pulling it back.

So one Saturday, he borrowed his neighbor's pressure washer and cleaned three driveways in his subdivision. Charged $75 each. Made $225 in five hours. He sat in his truck afterward, sweaty and tired, and realized he'd just made more in one afternoon than his extra payment for the entire month.

That was the day the math changed.

* * *

## You Can't Always Budget Your Way Out

Most debt books stop at spending. Cut this. Cancel that. Freeze your cards. Eat at home. All of that is necessary—you've already done it. But for a lot of families, cutting isn't enough. There's a floor to how low your expenses can go, and some of you are already standing on it.

You can't cut your rent. You can't cut your car payment without selling the car. You can't cut your electric bill to zero. Groceries have a minimum. Gas has a minimum. The necessities have a floor, and if your income barely clears that floor, the margin you're working with is thin. A hundred dollars. Maybe two hundred. That's real, and it matters, but it's not going to eliminate $20,000 in credit card debt in any timeframe that feels survivable.

This is the chapter most debt books don't write. Because talking about earning more is harder than talking about spending less. Spending less has a formula. Earning more has variables— your skills, your schedule, your energy, your market, your willingness to do something uncomfortable on a Saturday when you'd rather rest.

And there's something else nobody says out loud. It feels unfair. You already work hard. You already show up every day. The idea that you have to take on more—on top of the job, the kids, the household, the stress—can feel like the system is asking too much. And honestly, it is asking too much. But the debt doesn't care about fair. It charges interest whether you're resting or working. The only question is how long you want to carry it.

The math is undeniable. If you can bring in an extra $400 to $800 a month—even temporarily, even for six to twelve months—the speed of your debt payoff changes fundamentally. What felt like a three-year grind can compress to eighteen months or less. And that compression isn't just financial. It's emotional. It's the difference between a family that's tired and losing hope and a family that can see the end.

You're not looking for a career change. You're looking for a debt weapon. Something temporary, flexible, and real that puts extra dollars in your hands this month—not after a six-week certification or a $500 startup cost. This month.

* * *

## Fast Income vs. Long-Term Income

Before you start, understand the difference between these two categories. They both matter, but they serve different purposes in your reset.

**Fast income** is money you can make this week or this month with little to no setup. Selling unused items. Picking up a gig. Doing a service for a neighbor. It's not scalable and it's not permanent, but it puts cash in your hands immediately. During a debt reset, fast income is your accelerant. It's the extra $200 or $500 that turns a slow month into a month where the balance actually moves.

**Long-term income** is a side hustle or skill-based service you build over weeks or months that generates recurring revenue. Freelance work. A small service business. A weekend gig you can repeat. It takes more effort to start, but once it's running, it keeps producing. Long-term income is what sustains your payoff plan beyond the first burst of motivation.

The smartest approach is both. Start with fast income to create an immediate boost this month. While that money hits your target card, begin building one long-term income source that can carry you through the rest of the reset. You don't need five side hustles. You need one fast hit and one steady stream.

* * *

## Simple Side Income Ideas for Real Families

I'm not going to list thirty ideas and hope one sticks. I'm going to give you categories that work for working families—people who are already tired, already busy, and don't have startup capital to invest.

## Sell What You Already Own

This is the fastest money in this chapter. Walk through your house. Open the closets. Look in the garage. The treadmill nobody uses. The kids' outgrown clothes and toys. The electronics sitting in a drawer. The furniture from the room you reorganized two years ago.

Facebook Marketplace, OfferUp, and Craigslist are free to list on. Poshmark and Mercari work well for clothing and shoes. You're not building a business. You're liquidating dead inventory. Most families can pull $200 to $800 out of their house in the first two weeks if they're honest about what they're not using.

Keisha—Andre's wife—sold a stroller, a box of baby clothes, an old tablet, and a set of patio chairs in nine days on Facebook Marketplace. Total: $340. Every dollar went to the target card. She said the hardest part wasn't letting go of the stuff. It was admitting they'd spent money on things that had been sitting untouched for over a year.

## Service-Based Weekend Work

This is what Andre did with the pressure washer, and it's the most accessible category for most people. Service work doesn't require a degree, a website, or a business license in most cases. It requires a skill, some energy, and the willingness to knock on a door or post in a neighborhood group.

Pressure washing driveways and patios. Lawn mowing. Junk removal with a truck or trailer. Cleaning houses. Painting rooms. Assembling furniture. Hauling things to the dump. Hanging Christmas lights in November. Shoveling snow. Power-washing decks in the spring. None of these are glamorous. All of them pay cash, often the same day.

The going rate for most of these services ranges from $50 to $200 per job depending on your market. Two or three jobs on a Saturday can add $150 to $500 to your month. And the beauty of service work is that it scales with effort. If you need a bigger month because a setback hit, you book more jobs. If you need a lighter month, you pull back. It flexes with your life in a way that a part-time W-2 job doesn't.

Andre never advertised. He cleaned three driveways, and two of those neighbors told someone else. By the second month, people were texting him. He bought his own pressure washer for $280—which paid for itself in two jobs—and started doing patios and sidewalks too. He never worked more than one Saturday a month that he didn't choose to. It wasn't a business. It was a debt weapon with a trigger he could pull whenever he needed to.

## Skills-Based Gig Work

If you have a skill that people pay for—and most people do, even if they don't realize it—you can turn it into side income faster than you think.

You're good with numbers? Offer bookkeeping help to small businesses in your area. You can write clearly? Freelance on platforms like Upwork or Fiverr. You know your way around tools? Post handyman services on Nextdoor or TaskRabbit. You're organized? Offer to help people declutter, pack for a move, or set up a home office. You're bilingual? Translation and tutoring pay well and can be done from home.

The key is to start with what you already know. Don't spend three months learning a new skill to earn money you need this month. Use what's already in your hands. You can build new skills later, once the debt is under control and the pressure is off.

A woman named Theresa worked as an office manager during the week. Organized, efficient, good with spreadsheets. She didn't think of those as marketable skills until a friend asked her to help set up a filing system for her husband's small contracting business. Theresa spent a Sunday afternoon getting it organized and the friend paid her $150. She mentioned it on Nextdoor and within two weeks had three more small business owners asking for the same thing. By the end of the month, she'd made an extra $550 doing work she found easy—because it was something she already did every day for free.

That's the pattern to watch for. The thing you're good at—the thing people already come to you for—is probably worth money. You've just never charged for it.

* * *

## How to Avoid the Traps

When you're desperate to earn more, you become a target. And the internet is full of people who profit from that desperation.

Here are the red flags.

**If it requires you to pay money before you can earn money, walk away.** Starter kits. Training fees. "Investment opportunities." Legitimate work pays you. It doesn't charge you to start.

**If the income promise sounds too easy, it is.** "Make $5,000 a month from your phone" is a lie. "Earn $300 to $500 a month doing pressure washing on Saturdays" is real. The real opportunities sound boring. The scams sound exciting. That's by design.

**If someone recruits you to recruit other people, it's not a job.** Multi-level marketing companies target people in financial stress because the pitch sounds like a lifeline. It's not. The data on MLM earnings is brutal—the vast majority of participants lose money. Your time and energy are too valuable to invest in something with those odds during a debt reset.

Stick with things that have a clear exchange: you do a service, someone pays you. You sell an item, someone buys it. You complete a task, you get a check. Simple, direct, and honest. That's all you need right now.

One more thing. Be careful with gig apps that promise flexibility but eat your earnings in fees and expenses. Driving for rideshare sounds like easy money until you factor in gas, car wear, insurance, and the time between rides. Some people make it work. But do the real math before you commit your limited free hours. Calculate what you actually take home per hour after expenses—not the number the app shows you. If it's less than you'd make pressure-washing a driveway down the street, the driveway is the better bet.

* * *

## Where Every Extra Dollar Should Go

This is the rule that makes side income work as a debt strategy instead of just extra cash that dissolves into the month.

**Every dollar of side income goes directly to your target card. Every dollar. No exceptions.**

Not half. Not most of it. All of it. The side income is not for groceries. It's not for a night out because you worked hard. It's not for the thing you've been wanting to buy. It is debt ammunition and nothing else.

This is hard. I know it's hard. You just spent your Saturday pressure-washing driveways in the heat, and now you're supposed to send every cent of that to a credit card company. It feels like punishment. But here's the reframe: that money isn't going to the credit card company. It's buying back your future. Every dollar you send shortens the timeline. Every extra payment brings the day closer when you don't owe anyone anything.

Andre made a rule with Keisha. Every side dollar went to the card the same week it was earned. Not at the end of the month. That week. Because they both knew that money left sitting in checking for thirty days would find somewhere else to go. It always does. So he'd come home from a Saturday job, open the app, and make a payment that night. Sometimes it was $75. Sometimes it was $225. But it moved. And watching the balance respond in real time —not on a statement thirty days later, but that night—kept both of them in the game.

Over four months, Andre's Saturday pressure-washing jobs brought in just under $2,800. Combined with the $168 in monthly leak recovery and their $215 base margin, they were pushing over $900 a month toward their target card. The balance that was going to take three years started falling in months. By month five, the first card was paid off. The second one was already in range.

He didn't get a raise. He didn't change jobs. He didn't start a business. He borrowed a pressure washer and worked some Saturdays. That was enough.

* * *

## This Week's Reset

**One.** Walk through your house and identify at least ten items you can sell. Price them. List three of them today on Facebook Marketplace, OfferUp, or Poshmark. Don't wait until you have the perfect photos. List them.

**Two.** Write down three services you could offer in your neighborhood this month. Things you already know how to do. Pressure washing. Lawn care. Cleaning. Painting. Hauling. Organizing. Pick the one with the lowest barrier to entry and post it in a local Facebook group or on Nextdoor this week.

**Three.** If you have a marketable skill—writing, design, bookkeeping, tech support, tutoring, translation—create a free profile on one gig platform this week. Upwork, Fiverr, or TaskRabbit. You don't need to land a client today. You need to be visible so clients can find you.

**Four.** Set the rule now: every dollar of side income goes to the target card. Talk to your partner about it. Agree on it before the money comes in. Decisions made in advance hold up better than decisions made with cash in hand.

**Five.** Calculate your new total monthly debt weapon. Your Chapter 2 margin, plus your Chapter 5 recovered leaks, plus your estimated side income. Write that number down. Compare it to your minimum payments. For the first time, you're probably looking at a payoff timeline that feels like something you can survive.

You've stopped the bleeding. You've found the hidden money. Now you're bringing in new money. The 90-Day Family Debt Reset isn't about willpower. It's about stacking every advantage you can find until the math works in your favor.

Next chapter is Chapter 7—and if you haven't read it yet, it might be the most important one in the book. Because none of this works if the two people in your household can't talk about it without a fight.



## CHAPTER 7

# How to Talk About Debt Without Fighting

It was a Tuesday night. Nothing special about it. The kids were in bed. The dishes were done. And Lisa was sitting at the kitchen table with a credit card statement she'd been hiding in her car for eleven days.

She didn't plan to hide it. But when the envelope came and she saw the balance—$7,400 on a card her husband Marcus didn't know about—she froze. Most of it was groceries, the kids' dentist, a car repair from October. Normal stuff. Stuff they needed. But she already knew what Marcus would say.

"Why didn't you tell me?"

That question—the one that sounds reasonable but lands like an accusation—is why millions of families don't talk about debt at all. Not because they don't care. Because they're afraid of what happens when they do.

* * *

## Debt Is Emotional Before It Is Financial

Most money books skip this part. They hand you a spreadsheet and a payoff calculator and act like the hard part is math. It's not. The hard part is sitting across from someone you love and saying things are worse than they thought.

Debt carries shame. The quiet kind. The kind that sits in your chest when you check your phone for a balance alert in the bathroom so nobody sees your face. The kind that makes you pay for dinner with one card because the other got declined last week. The kind that makes you say "we're fine" when your sister asks how things are going, and then you go sit in the car for a minute before driving home.

That shame doesn't go away when you make a budget. It goes away when someone sees it and doesn't judge you for it.

That's why this chapter matters more than the payoff strategies or the spending freeze. If you and your partner can't talk about money without it turning into a fight, none of the other chapters will stick. You'll make a plan on Sunday and abandon it by Wednesday because one person felt controlled and the other felt ignored.

This isn't a communication chapter. This is a survival chapter.

* * *

## Why Couples Fight About Money

Money fights aren't really about money. They're about fear, control, trust, and the stories we grew up with.

Think about how you learned about money as a kid. Maybe your parents fought about it behind closed doors and you heard every word through the wall. Maybe your mom stretched $40 into a week of groceries. Maybe your dad spent freely and nobody questioned it. Whatever you saw, that's your money story. And your partner has a completely different one.

One of you might be a saver who checks the bank app three times a day. The other might avoid looking at it for weeks because the number makes their stomach hurt. One of you deals with stress by making spreadsheets. The other deals with it by pretending the problem isn't there yet.

Neither of you is wrong. But when you're both exhausted and $22,000 deep in credit card debt, those differences stop being personality traits and start feeling personal.

"You spent $180 at Target?"

"You never let me buy anything."

"I'm the only one who cares about this."

Those aren't budget arguments. They're fear talking. And if you keep having them the same way, you'll keep getting the same result: silence, resentment, or an explosion. None of which pay off a single dollar.

* * *

## The Weekly Money Check-In

You don't need a three-hour financial summit. You need twenty minutes, once a week, same day, same time.

Call it whatever works. The reset. The check-in. Tuesday money time. The name doesn't matter. The consistency does.

Here's what a good one looks like.

**Pick a calm time.** Not when the kids are screaming. Not right after work. Sunday morning with coffee works for some couples. Wednesday after bedtime works for others. Find your window and protect it.

**Start with a win.** Before you look at a single number, each person shares one thing that went well with money that week. Maybe you packed lunch instead of buying it. Maybe you didn't use the credit card. It sounds small. It changes the whole energy.

**Look at the numbers together.** Pull up the balances. Check what came in, what went out. If a number is higher than expected, don't react. Ask what happened. Not with suspicion. With curiosity.

**Talk about the week ahead.** Any big expenses coming? Birthdays, bills, car stuff? Seeing it early means planning instead of panicking.

**End with agreement, not assignment.**
There's a difference between "you need to stop eating out" and "let's try to cook four nights this week." One sounds like a parent. The other sounds like a partner.

That's it. Twenty minutes.

A couple I know—James and Tanya—were $31,000 in credit card debt when they started doing weekly check-ins. Tanya said the first three were rough. James sat at the table with his arms crossed and barely looked at her. She'd pull up the spreadsheet on her laptop and talk through the numbers while he stared at the wall behind her head. She told me she almost quit after week two because it felt like performing a monologue in her own kitchen.

But she kept showing up. By week five, something shifted. He started bringing his own notes—just a scrap of paper with a few things written down, but it meant he'd been thinking about it between check-ins. By week eight, he was the one reminding her it was Tuesday. She said later that what changed wasn't the system.

It was that he finally believed she wasn't going to use the numbers against him.

When you talk about money every week, you never go long enough for things to build up. There's nothing to hide. Nothing to explode about. It just becomes part of how your household works.

* * *

## What to Say When Blame Shows Up

Blame is the fastest way to kill a money conversation.

When you see a charge you didn't expect, your gut doesn't say "let me ask about this calmly." Your gut says "what the hell did you buy now?" That's not because you're a bad partner. Debt makes everything feel urgent, and urgency makes people mean. You know that feeling—you hear your own voice go sharp and part of you wants to pull it back, but the words are already out.

Reacting doesn't solve anything. It just teaches the other person to hide things next time.

**Pause before you speak.** Count to five. That tiny gap between the feeling and the words is where you choose whether this becomes a conversation or a fight.

**Replace "you" with "we."** Instead of "you spent too much on groceries," try "we went over on groceries—what happened this week?" "You" points a finger. "We" opens a door.

**Name the feeling, not the accusation.** Instead of "you don't care about our debt," try "I'm feeling really stressed about where we are right now." One invites defensiveness. The other invites honesty.

**Ask before assuming.** That $90 charge at the auto parts store might be your partner fixing the brake light themselves to save on a mechanic. But if you come in hot, you'll never hear that. You'll just hear the door close.

I know this is hard. You're not in a therapist's office. You're standing in your kitchen at 9 PM, tired, looking at numbers that make your stomach hurt. Nobody speaks perfectly in that moment.

If you catch yourself blaming, stop. Say "I'm sorry. That came out wrong. Let me try again." You don't have to get it right every time. You just have to be willing to correct it when you don't.

* * *

## When One Partner Won't Engage

Some of you are reading this alone. Your partner doesn't want to look at the numbers. Changes the subject. Gets angry when you bring it up. Maybe they say "I'll handle it" and nothing changes.

You can't force someone to engage. But you can change the conditions that make them avoid it.

Most people who refuse to talk about debt aren't being stubborn. They're overwhelmed. They feel like every conversation is going to end with them being the problem. Or they've tried before and nothing changed, so talking feels pointless. Some people shut down because that's how they survived money stress growing up—nobody in their house talked about it either.

**Lower the stakes.** Don't sit them down for a "big talk." That phrase alone makes people shut off. Instead: "Hey, I think we're overpaying on the phone bill. Want to look at it together for five minutes?" Small door. Easy to walk through.

**Share your fear first.** Instead of "we need to talk about our debt," try "I've been stressed about money and I don't want to carry that alone. Can I just tell you where I'm at?" You're not asking them to perform. You're asking them to listen.

**Show progress, not problems.** If you've already started working through this book, show a small win. "I found $80 in subscriptions we weren't using. Already canceled." When someone sees that the work actually produces results, they're more likely to lean in.

**Don't weaponize the book.** Do not leave this book on your partner's nightstand with a sticky note. Don't quote chapters at them during an argument. Don't say "the book says we should do check-ins and you're refusing." That's not motivation. That's ammunition.

If your partner truly won't engage after weeks of consistent, gentle effort, that might be a counseling conversation, not a budget conversation. That's okay. Getting help means you care enough to protect the relationship while you fix the money.

* * *

## How to Reset as a Team

Paying off debt as a couple will test your relationship. Not because of the money. Because of what the money reveals about both of you.

Who handles pressure. Who avoids it. Who holds grudges. Who shuts down. You'll see parts of each other you didn't expect, and some of it will be uncomfortable. There might be a night where one of you stares at the ceiling wondering if this is going to work. That's normal. That's the middle of the process, not the end of it.

Couples who get through this together come out closer. Not because the debt disappears. Because they stopped fighting each other and started fighting the same problem.

So before you get deep into the payoff plan, sit down and agree on a few ground rules. Not a contract. Not a lecture. Just some honest agreements about how you're going to operate from here.

**Drop the scorecard.** I know you remember who ran up the Visa. I know you remember the $600 they spent on something stupid last March. Let it go. Not because it doesn't matter, but because keeping score turns your partner into an opponent. You can't pay off debt with someone you're keeping a case against.

**No more financial secrets.** This one is simple and it's hard. Full transparency going forward. That doesn't mean texting each other a receipt for every coffee. It means no hidden cards. No secret accounts. No charges you'd panic about if they showed up on the screen during a check-in. If you wouldn't say it out loud, don't do it quietly.

**Both of you sacrifice something.** This falls apart fast when one person gives things up and the other keeps living the same way. Resentment builds in silence and then it comes out sideways—usually during a check-in about something unrelated. Both partners cut back. Not necessarily the same things, but enough that neither one feels punished while the other skates by.

**Say the wins out loud.** When a card gets paid off, don't just move on to the next one. Stop. Look at each other. "We did that." It takes three seconds and it matters more than you'd think after weeks of saying no to things you wanted.

Marcus and Lisa—from the beginning of this chapter—eventually had the conversation. It wasn't smooth. She cried. He sat there for a long time not saying anything. She said it felt like the longest silence of her life.

Then he said something she didn't expect.

"I wish you'd told me. Not because I'm mad. Because you carried that alone and you didn't have to."

That's what a reset sounds like. Not scripted. Not clean. Just two people deciding the debt isn't going to be a wall between them anymore.

* * *

## This Week's Reset

**One.** Pick a day and time for your first money check-in. Put it on the calendar. Treat it like an appointment.

**Two.** Before the check-in, each person writes down one money win from the week. Even if it's small.

**Three.** During the check-in, pull up all your credit card balances together. No hiding. No guessing. Just the numbers on the table.

**Four.** If blame comes up, practice the swap. Replace "you" with "we." Just that one thing.

**Five.** End by agreeing on one thing you'll do differently next week. Just one. Build from there.

You don't have to fix your finances tonight. You just have to start talking about them without making each other the enemy.

And if the first check-in is awkward, good. Awkward means you showed up. That counts more than you think.



## CHAPTER 8

# Build Your Family Debt Rules.

Dana and Malik paid off their first credit card on a Wednesday night in October. They'd been working the hybrid method for eleven weeks. Dana had picked up extra shifts at the hospital. Malik had sold the weight bench, the old laptop, and a stack of Jordan boxes he'd been holding onto for years. They'd run the leak audit, cut four subscriptions, switched phone plans. And that Wednesday, the Visa hit zero.

They celebrated. Ordered pizza. Felt like they'd won something real.

By the following Tuesday, Malik had bought a pair of shoes online. Not expensive—$85. But he put them on the card. The one they'd just paid off. He didn't think about it. The card was empty, the shoes were on sale, and the old habit kicked in before the new one had time to stick.

Dana found out when she checked the balance the next morning. She didn't yell. She just went quiet. And that silence carried more weight than any argument could have.

They talked about it that night. Not a big fight—they'd learned how to avoid that in Phase 2. But an honest conversation about what happened. Malik said he didn't even think about it. The card was free, the purchase was small, and the old muscle memory just fired. Dana said she understood, but that watching the zero disappear after everything they'd done to reach it felt like a gut punch. The problem wasn't the shoes. The problem was that they had a plan for paying off debt but no plan for what happened after a card was paid off.

They didn't have a spending rule. They had momentum. And momentum without rules is just energy waiting to run out.

* * *

## Rules Remove Pressure

Most people think rules are restrictive. They associate them with being told what to do—budgets they can't follow, diets that make them miserable, spending limits that feel like a punishment handed down by whichever partner is "better with money."

But good rules don't restrict. They decide in advance. And deciding in advance is the single most powerful thing a household can do to protect its progress during a debt reset.

Think about it. Without a rule, every spending decision becomes a negotiation. Should we eat out tonight? Can I buy this? Do we have room for that? Each of those conversations carries weight. Each one has the potential to turn into tension, judgment, or a fight. You're standing in the cereal aisle wondering if the $6 granola is within bounds or if you should grab the $3 store brand, and the real question isn't about cereal— it's about whether you're going to feel guilty when you get home. After eight or ten of those micro-decisions in a week, you're not thinking clearly anymore. You're just tired. And tired people default to old habits.

Rules eliminate the negotiation. If you've already agreed that anything over $50 gets discussed first, then when Malik sees those shoes, the decision is already made. He doesn't have to wrestle with it. He doesn't have to wonder if Dana will be upset. The rule says: text her first. Talk about it. If it fits the plan, buy it. If it doesn't, wait.

That's not control. That's a system. And systems work when willpower doesn't.

* * *

## Create Your Family Money Code

Your Family Money Code is a short set of rules —no more than five to seven—that your household agrees to follow during the 90-Day Family Debt Reset and beyond. These aren't aspirations. They're operating agreements. They're how your family handles money from this point forward.

Here's how to build yours.

Sit down together. If you've been doing the weekly money check-ins from Chapter 7, use that time. If not, pick a calm evening. This conversation should take about thirty minutes.

Start with what's already gone wrong. Not to assign blame—to identify the gaps. Malik buying the shoes wasn't a character flaw. It was the absence of a rule for how they'd use a card after paying it off. Dana's silence wasn't an overreaction. It was the natural response to a system failure when no system existed.

Ask each other: where have we slipped? Where have we disagreed about spending? Where has one person felt controlled and the other felt ignored? Those friction points are where your rules need to live.

Then write them down. Together. In plain language that a twelve-year-old could understand. No financial jargon. No complicated formulas. Rules only work if both people can remember them without checking a document.

Dana and Malik wrote theirs on a Sunday evening after the boys were in bed. Dana wanted ten rules. Malik wanted three. They negotiated to six. The conversation took longer than the actual writing—about forty minutes of talking through what had tripped them up, what felt fair, and what each of them needed to feel respected in the process. By the time they wrote the final list, both of them felt ownership over it. That's the key. Rules imposed by one partner get resisted by the other. Rules built together get followed by both.

Here are examples of strong family money rules. Yours don't have to match these—but they should be this specific.

**The $50 rule.** Any non-essential purchase over $50 gets discussed before it happens. Not approved—discussed. The goal is awareness, not permission. If both people agree it fits, buy it. If one person has concerns, wait 48 hours and revisit. Most impulse purchases don't survive a 48-hour pause.

**The zero-balance rule.** Any credit card that reaches a zero balance stays at zero. It doesn't get used for new purchases. It doesn't become the "emergency" card. It's done. This is the rule Dana and Malik needed—and the one that would have prevented an $85 relapse and a week of tension.

**The same-day rule for side income.** Any extra money earned outside regular paychecks gets sent to the target card the same day or same week it's received. It doesn't sit in checking. It doesn't get absorbed. It moves immediately.

**The weekly reset.** Every week, during your check-in, review the rules together. Not to police each other. To stay aligned. People drift.

Rules get fuzzy after a few weeks. The check-in keeps them sharp.

**The emergency definition.** You already built this in Chapter 3. Keep it active. If the spending freeze has loosened—and it naturally will by month three—revisit your emergency list and make sure both of you still agree on what qualifies.

* * *

## When to Say Yes and When to Say No

Rules aren't about saying no to everything. A reset that runs on pure deprivation will collapse. You know that because you've probably tried it before—the diet where you cut everything, white-knuckled it for three weeks, and then ate an entire pizza at midnight because your body and brain revolted.

Money works the same way. If the rules feel like a cage, someone is going to break out. And they usually break out in the worst possible way—a big purchase, hidden spending, or a fight that undoes weeks of progress.

So your rules need breathing room.

The weekly cash allowance from Chapter 3? Keep it. Maybe increase it slightly now that you're in Phase 3 and your payoff plan has traction. If $25 a week was the freeze amount, maybe $35 works now. That's an extra $40 a month total for two adults. It's not going to derail your payoff plan, and it keeps both people from feeling like they're living in a financial straitjacket.

Birthdays and holidays will come. Kids will need things. Your car will need tires eventually. The point of the rules isn't to pretend those things don't exist. It's to plan for them. When you know a birthday is two weeks away, you put $30 aside from the weekly budget over those two weeks. When you know the tires are getting thin, you start a small sinking fund—even $20 a paycheck. Chapter 10 goes deeper on this, but the principle starts here: expected expenses should never feel like emergencies.

Here's a practical way to handle it. At the beginning of each month, during your first weekly check-in, look ahead at the calendar together. What's coming? A birthday. A school field trip fee. A car registration renewal. An annual subscription that hits once a year. Write down every known expense and its approximate cost. Then divide that total across the month's paychecks. That money gets set aside before anything else—before the target card payment, before the discretionary spending. Because if you don't plan for it, it becomes a "surprise" that goes on the credit card, and you're right back where you started.

Say yes to planned spending. Say no to unplanned spending that doesn't meet the emergency definition. That simple filter handles about 80 percent of the decisions your household will face.

* * *

## The Power of a Weekly Reset Rhythm

By now you should be several weeks into your weekly money check-ins. If they're working, you already know the rhythm: start with a win, look at the numbers, talk about the week ahead, agree on one thing.

In Phase 3, the check-in evolves. It's no longer just about reviewing balances. It's about reviewing the rules.

Every week, take two minutes at the end of your check-in and ask each other: did we follow the rules this week? Not in a way that sounds like a report card. In a way that sounds like two people tuning an instrument. Small adjustments. Honest answers.

Maybe the $50 rule worked perfectly, but you realized it should be $75 for groceries because that's where most of the spending happens and $50 is too low to be practical. Adjust it. Maybe the same-day rule for side income slipped because Malik forgot to transfer the money on Saturday and it sat in checking until Tuesday. Recommit. Maybe the emergency definition needs updating because the car situation changed.

Rules that don't get reviewed become rules that don't get followed. The weekly check-in is where they stay alive.

Dana told me that their rules didn't feel real until the third week. The first two weeks, they were just words on a piece of paper. By week three, they'd had to use them twice—once when Malik wanted to buy a jacket and once when Dana wanted to sign up for a fitness app. Both times, the $50 rule kicked in. Both times, they talked about it. Both times, they waited 48 hours. Malik ended up buying the jacket because it replaced one that was falling apart. Dana decided the app wasn't worth it. The rules didn't say no. The rules made the decision deliberate instead of automatic.

That's the difference between a household running on rules and a household running on willpower. Willpower fades. Rules hold.

* * *

## How Rules Protect Peace

There's a reason this chapter comes right after Chapter 7. The communication chapter taught you how to talk about money without fighting. This chapter gives you a structure that reduces how often you need to have hard conversations at all.

When there's no rule, every financial decision is a conversation. And not all conversations happen at good times. You're tired. The kids are loud. Someone's already in a bad mood. One poorly timed question about a charge on the statement can spiral into a thirty-minute argument that has nothing to do with the actual purchase and everything to do with the stress sitting underneath it.

Rules absorb that stress. If the rule says anything over $50 gets discussed, then the discussion isn't triggered by suspicion or annoyance—it's triggered by the system. Nobody is being policed. Nobody is the money cop. The rule is the cop. And the rule doesn't have an attitude or a tone of voice.

This matters especially in households where one partner handles most of the finances. Without rules, that person becomes the gatekeeper—and the other person starts to feel like a kid asking for an allowance. It breeds resentment on both sides. The person managing the money feels like they carry all the responsibility. The other person feels like they've lost autonomy.

Shared rules fix that. When both people built the code together, neither one is imposing it on the other. You're both accountable to the same agreement. That shifts the dynamic from parent-child to partners. And partnerships survive debt. Parent-child dynamics don't.

Something else happens when you have clear rules: the stress in the house drops. Not just between you and your partner. The whole household feels it. Kids pick up on financial tension even when you think you're hiding it. They notice the pause when they ask for something. They hear the tone shift when a bill comes up. When the adults in the house have a system they both trust, that tension fades. You can say "not this week" to your kid without it carrying the weight of the entire debt behind it.

Because you know—and they sense—that there's a plan. It's not chaos. It's a choice.

Malik said something about three months in that stuck with me. He said, "The rules made it so I didn't have to ask Dana for permission. I just had to check the system we agreed on. That changed everything for me." He wasn't asking to spend money. He was checking whether the spending fit the agreement. Same outcome. Completely different feeling.

* * *

## This Week's Reset

**One.** Sit down with your partner and write your Family Money Code. Five to seven rules. Plain language. Based on where you've slipped, where you've argued, and what you've learned through the first two phases. If you're doing this alone, write the rules for yourself. They work the same way.

**Two.** Include at minimum: a spending threshold that triggers discussion, a zero-balance rule for paid-off cards, a same-day transfer rule for extra income, and a commitment to the weekly check-in.

**Three.** Put the rules somewhere visible. The fridge. A shared notes app. Taped inside the kitchen cabinet. They need to live where you'll see them on a Tuesday afternoon when a purchase decision comes up—not buried in a notebook on a shelf.

**Four.** During this week's check-in, review the rules together for the first time. Adjust anything that doesn't feel right. The first version doesn't have to be final. It just has to be agreed on.

**Five.** Revisit your weekly cash allowance. If the Phase 1 amount feels too tight now that your payoff plan has traction, give yourself a small increase. Sustainability matters more than speed. A rule you can follow for six months beats a rule you abandon in three weeks.

Phase 3 is about protecting what you've built. The spending freeze was temporary. The leak audit was a one-time exercise. But the rules—if you commit to them—become the way your household operates from here on. Not just until the debt is gone. After.

Next chapter: what to do when life hits back. Because it will. And the plan you've built needs to survive it.



## CHAPTER 9

# Handle Setbacks Without Giving Up.

They were four months in. Two cards paid off. Weekly check-ins running smooth. The target card was down to $4,100 from $7,800. Andre and Keisha—the couple from Chapter 6—had found their rhythm. The pressure-washing money was coming in. The spending freeze had loosened into a set of family rules they could live with. For the first time in years, they felt like the debt was losing.

Then the transmission went out.

$2,700. The mechanic showed Andre the damage and gave him two options: fix it or junk the car. He drove that car to work every day. Without it, there was no paycheck. Without the paycheck, there was no payoff plan. There was nothing.

Andre called Keisha from the shop parking lot. He was standing next to the car with the hood still up, grease on the estimate sheet, sweat on the back of his neck. She could hear it in his voice before he said a word. They sat on the phone in silence for a few seconds. Then she said, "What do we do?"

And that question—asked calmly, without blame, without panic—is the reason this chapter exists.

* * *

## Setbacks Don't Mean Failure

Every family paying off debt will get hit. Not might. Will. The question was never whether a setback was coming. The question is what you do when it arrives.

Car repairs. Medical bills. A job change. A furnace in February. A kid who breaks an arm at practice. A family emergency that requires a last-minute plane ticket. Life doesn't check your payoff plan before sending you a bill. It just sends it.

And here's what happens to most families when the hit lands. They look at the new expense, compare it to the progress they've made, and feel the whole thing collapsing. Four months of sacrifice, and one car repair just ate three months of extra payments. The math is so discouraging that the emotional response takes over: what's the point?

That moment—the "what's the point" moment—is where most debt payoff plans die. Not because the setback was too big. Because the family didn't have a plan for how to survive it emotionally. The spreadsheet can handle a setback. You add the new expense, adjust the timeline, recalculate. The math still works. But the human being staring at the spreadsheet sometimes can't absorb what the numbers are telling them. Three months of sacrifice, erased by something you didn't choose and couldn't prevent. It feels cruel. It feels like the universe saw you trying and decided to test whether you meant it.

You meant it. And the test isn't whether the setback happens. The test is whether you're still here after it does.

So let me say this as plainly as I can. A setback is not a reset. It's not a sign that the plan doesn't work. It's not proof that your family can't do this. It's a bad month. Maybe two bad months. And then you keep going. The families who pay off serious debt aren't the ones who never got hit. They're the ones who got hit and didn't stop.

* * *

## What to Do After a Financial Hit

When a big unexpected expense lands, your brain wants to react immediately. Fix it. Solve it. Make the panic stop. That instinct is useful in emergencies—but it's terrible for financial decisions. Panic spending always costs more than planned spending.

Here's a better sequence.

**Step one: Stop and assess.** Before you swipe a card or write a check, understand the full scope of the expense. How much is it? Is there any flexibility in the cost? Can you negotiate a payment plan directly with the provider? Most mechanics, hospitals, and service providers will let you break a large bill into payments—often interest-free—if you ask before paying. Most people don't ask.

**Step two: Check your options.** Can the repair wait a few days while you get a second quote? Is there a less expensive fix that buys you time? For medical bills, can you negotiate the amount down or apply for financial assistance through the hospital? Many hospitals have programs that reduce bills significantly for families below a certain income threshold—programs they don't advertise. You have to ask.

**Step three: Decide how to pay.** This is where the old you and the new you diverge. The old you puts the whole thing on the credit card and worries about it later. The new you has options. Can you cover part of it with cash and put the rest on a payment plan? Can you temporarily reduce your extra debt payment this month and redirect that money toward the emergency? Can you pick up extra side work this week to cover the gap?

**Step four: Adjust the plan, don't abandon it.** This is the most important step. A setback might mean your extra payment drops from $400 to $100 this month. Fine. It might mean you pause the extra payment entirely for one month while you handle the crisis. That's okay too. What you don't do is stop the minimums. What you don't do is cancel the check-in. What you don't do is close the spreadsheet and decide the whole thing was pointless.

Andre and Keisha worked the steps. The mechanic offered a payment plan: $500 up front and four monthly payments of $550. They used $500 from their emergency stash—money they'd started setting aside in small amounts since Phase 1. Their extra debt payment dropped from $900 to $350 for four months while they handled the transmission. It wasn't ideal. The payoff timeline stretched by about three months. But the plan survived. And so did they.

* * *

## How to Recover From a Bad Month

Not every setback is a $2,700 transmission. Sometimes the bad month is quieter. You overspent on groceries three weeks in a row. The kids needed winter coats and shoes at the same time. Someone used the credit card when they shouldn't have—not a lot, maybe $200— and didn't say anything until the statement came.

These small setbacks don't feel like emergencies, but they're actually more dangerous. Because they don't trigger the crisis response. They just erode progress quietly. A $200 charge here. A missed extra payment there. A month where you meant to send $400 to the target card but only managed $80. None of those feel catastrophic in the moment. But string three of them together and you've lost a quarter of real progress.

Here's how to handle a bad month without letting it become a bad quarter.

**Name it at the check-in.** Don't pretend it didn't happen. Don't wait for your partner to notice. Bring it up. "This month didn't go the way we planned. Here's what happened." That sentence alone prevents the silence and hiding that let small slips become big ones.

**Diagnose it.** Was it a spending problem, an income problem, or an unexpected expense? Each one has a different fix. A spending slip means your rules need tightening or your allowance needs adjusting. An income drop means you look at side work options from Chapter 6. An unexpected expense means you need to build your emergency cushion faster— Chapter 10 is coming.

**Make next month the recovery month.** Don't try to make up everything in one paycheck. Spread the recovery over the next thirty days. If you fell $300 short on the extra payment, add $75 a week for the next four weeks. If a card charge slipped through, focus the first week's side income entirely on paying that off. Small, steady corrections beat dramatic overcorrections that burn you out.

A woman I worked with—let's call her Priya—had been doing everything right for three months. Then her daughter's school sent home a list of expenses: field trip, class photos, yearbook, science fair supplies. None of them were optional in her daughter's eyes. Total came to about $165. Not a crisis. But it pushed her over budget, she used the card, and then she felt so frustrated with herself that she skipped the next two check-ins because she didn't want to see the numbers.

Two skipped check-ins turned into two months of drift. Not because $165 derailed her plan. Because the guilt about $165 made her avoid the system that would have kept her on track. She stopped looking at the banking app. She stopped updating the spreadsheet. She ordered takeout twice because she was exhausted from feeling bad about the spending, which is the kind of irony that debt creates—stress spending caused by the stress of having spent. When she finally sat down and looked at the numbers again, she'd lost about $600 in progress. Not from the school expenses. From the spending that crept back in while she wasn't watching.

The lesson isn't "don't feel guilty." Guilt is natural. The lesson is: don't let guilt keep you from showing up. The check-in after a bad month is the most important check-in you'll have. Skipping it is how small setbacks become big ones.

* * *

## The Bounce-Back Plan

Every family in this process needs a bounce-back plan before the setback arrives. Not after. Before. Because in the middle of a crisis, you don't have the bandwidth to think clearly about money strategy. You're just trying to get through the week.

Here's what a bounce-back plan looks like. Write this down and keep it with your debt snapshot and your Family Money Code.

**If the setback is under $500:** Cover it from your current month's budget by temporarily reducing your extra debt payment. Don't touch the emergency fund for small hits—that fund is for the bigger stuff. Recover the difference over the next two to four weeks through tighter spending or one extra side job.

**If the setback is $500 to $2,000:** Use your emergency fund if you have one. Negotiate a payment plan with the provider. Reduce your extra debt payment to minimums-only for one to two months while you stabilize. Pick up additional side income specifically to cover the gap. Resume full extra payments as soon as the emergency expense is handled.

**If the setback is over $2,000:** Use every tool available. Emergency fund, payment plan negotiation, reduced debt payments, increased side income. Accept that your payoff timeline is going to shift by two to four months. That's not failure—that's reality. Adjust your tracking numbers, update your debt snapshot, and keep moving forward from the new position.

The critical thing in all three tiers: you don't stop. You adjust the pace, but the direction stays the same. The check-ins continue. The rules stay active. The target card still gets something, even if it's just the minimum for a month.

Stopping is the one thing you can't recover from quickly. Slowing down is fine. Pausing the extra payment for a month is fine. But if you close the spreadsheet, cancel the check-ins, and go back to guessing—that's when months of progress disappear. Not because of the setback. Because you left the system that was protecting you.

Think of it like this. If you're driving from Ohio to Nevada and you get a flat tire in Indiana, you don't turn around and go home. You fix the tire and keep driving. Maybe you arrive a few hours later than planned. But you still arrive. The families who pay off debt aren't the ones with no flat tires. They're the ones who fix the tire and keep driving.

*  *  *

## Progress Beats Perfection

I want to say something to the reader who's already had a bad month. Maybe more than one.

Maybe you're reading this chapter after falling off the plan for six weeks, and you're not sure if it's worth picking back up.

It is.

You don't have to go back to the beginning. You don't have to redo Phase 1. You don't have to rebuild your snapshot from scratch or re-read every chapter. Pull up your last debt snapshot. Update the numbers. Look at where you are right now. That's your new starting line. Set the check-in for this week. Follow your rules. Make one extra payment, even a small one. You're back in.

The families who fail at paying off debt aren't the ones who have setbacks. Every family has setbacks. The ones who fail are the ones who interpret the setback as evidence that they can't do it. They tell themselves a story: we're just not disciplined enough, we make too little, we'll never get out. And then the story becomes the plan—which is no plan at all.

Don't let a bad month write your story.

Andre told me later that the transmission felt like the worst moment of the entire process. Worse than seeing the initial debt total. Worse than the first spending freeze. Because this time, he had something to lose. He'd built real progress, and watching it get swallowed by one repair bill felt personal. Like the universe was punishing him for trying.

But they kept the check-ins going. They kept the rules active. They adjusted the extra payment and worked the payment plan with the mechanic. Four months later, the transmission was paid off. Five months after that, the last credit card hit zero.

The setback added about three months to their timeline. That's it. Three months. Against a problem that could have ended the whole process if they'd let it.

Progress doesn't require perfection. It requires you to keep showing up after the months that don't go as planned. That's the whole game.

* * *

## This Week's Reset

**One.** Write your bounce-back plan. Three tiers: under $500, $500 to $2,000, over $2,000. Keep it with your debt snapshot. You want this ready before you need it, not while you're panicking in a mechanic's parking lot.

**Two.** If you've had a setback recently, update your debt snapshot this week. Don't avoid the numbers. Face them the same way you did in Chapter 2. Write down the new total. That's your current starting line.

**Three.** If you've skipped check-ins, restart them this week. The first one back might be uncomfortable. Do it anyway. The check-in after a bad month is the one that matters most.

**Four.** Talk to your partner about how you want to handle the next hit. Not if—when. Agree in advance on the approach: negotiate first, use the emergency fund if needed, adjust the extra payment temporarily, and keep the system running.

**Five.** Remind yourself where you started. Pull up your original debt snapshot from Chapter 2.

Compare it to where you are now—even after the setback. If the number is lower, you're winning. Slowly, imperfectly, and with interruptions. But winning.

Setbacks are part of the process. Not a detour from it. The 90-Day Family Debt Reset doesn't promise you a smooth road. It promises you a system that holds up when the road gets rough.

Next chapter: how to make sure you never end up back here. Protection isn't about hoping for the best. It's about building the safety nets that catch you before you fall.



CHAPTER 10

# Protect Your Finances From Future Damage.

The last time Monique's car needed work—about two years before she started the 90-Day Family Debt Reset—she put the whole thing on her Mastercard. Didn't think twice. The mechanic said $840, she handed over the card, and it went on the pile with everything else. She didn't have another option.

Eight months into the reset, her car needed work again. Different problem, similar cost: $780. But this time, something was different. She had $1,100 sitting in a separate savings account she'd been building since month two. Twenty dollars here. Fifty dollars there. A small automatic transfer every payday that she barely noticed leaving her checking account.

She paid the mechanic in cash. Drove home. Sat in her driveway for a minute. And then she cried —not from stress, but from relief. For the first time in years, an emergency didn't become debt. The system worked. And she didn't have to undo a single month of progress to handle it.

This chapter is about building that system. The one that catches you before a setback sends you backward. Because paying off debt without building protection is like putting out a fire and leaving the matches on the table. The work isn't done when the balance hits zero. The work is done when the next emergency comes and the credit card stays in the drawer.

# Debt Freedom Needs Protection

Paying off credit card debt is hard. Staying out of it is a different challenge entirely. And most books treat it like an afterthought—a final chapter about "smart habits" that reads like a motivational poster.

This isn't that chapter.

The reality is simple and uncomfortable: the same life that put you into debt is still happening. The car will break down again. The medical bills will come again. The furnace, the roof, the dental emergency—they're all still out there, on their own timeline, indifferent to your payoff plan. If you don't build protection between your family and those expenses, you'll end up right back where you started. Not because you failed. Because you didn't build a wall.

Chapter 8 gave you internal rules for how your household operates. This chapter is about external infrastructure—the financial structures you put in place outside your daily spending that absorb the shocks before they reach your credit card.

Think of it this way. The Family Money Code from Chapter 8 is how you drive. This chapter is the seatbelt, the airbags, and the insurance. You hope you never need them. But when you do, they're the difference between a bad day and a disaster.

* * *

## Your First Safety Net

You've heard the advice: save three to six months of expenses in an emergency fund. That's good advice for someone who isn't carrying $20,000 in credit card debt. For you, right now, that number is unrealistic and unhelpful. If you could save $15,000, you wouldn't be reading this book.

So let's talk about what you can actually do.

Your first safety net is a starter emergency fund. Not three months. Not six months. One thousand dollars. That's the target. Enough to cover a car repair, a medical copay, a broken appliance, or a last-minute expense that would otherwise go on the card. It won't cover everything. It doesn't have to. It just has to cover the most common emergencies that derail families mid-payoff.

Here's how to build it without slowing down your debt payoff.

**Set up an automatic transfer.** Every payday, move a small amount—$20, $30, $50, whatever you can manage—into a separate savings account. Not your main checking. A different account. One you don't check daily. One that isn't linked to your debit card. The goal is to make the money invisible to your daily spending. If you don't see it, you won't spend it.

**Use a high-yield savings account if you can.** Online banks often offer rates ten to fifteen times higher than traditional banks. On $1,000, the difference isn't life-changing—maybe $40 to $50 a year in interest. But it's free money on money that's already sitting there. And psychologically, watching the balance grow even by a few cents each month reinforces the habit.

**Don't touch it for non-emergencies.** This is the hard one. The emergency fund is not for Christmas gifts. It's not for a weekend trip. It's not for a sale that ends tonight. It exists for one purpose: keeping an unexpected expense off the credit card. Use the same emergency definition you built in Chapter 3. If it doesn't meet that definition, the fund stays untouched.

Monique built her $1,100 fund in about seven months. She started with $25 per paycheck. After the Chapter 5 leak audit freed up more cash, she bumped it to $50. She never missed the money because it left her account automatically before she had a chance to allocate it. By the time the car repair hit, she'd almost forgotten the account existed. That was the point.

A thousand dollars won't solve every problem. But it solves the most common one: the unexpected $400 to $900 expense that sends a family back to the credit card and undoes months of work. With a starter fund in place, that expense becomes an inconvenience instead of a crisis.

## Why Every Family Needs Sinking Funds

The emergency fund handles the surprises. Sinking funds handle the expenses you can see coming but tend to forget about until they arrive.

Car registration. Annual insurance premiums. Back-to-school shopping. Holiday gifts. The dentist visit that happens every six months. The summer camp deposit that's due in April. Your kid's birthday party. These aren't emergencies. They're predictable. But most families treat them like emergencies because they don't set money aside in advance. The bill shows up, there's no cash for it, and out comes the card.

A sinking fund is just money you set aside each month for a known future expense. You divide the total cost by the number of months until it's due, and you save that amount every month. When the expense arrives, the money is already there.

You don't need a separate bank account for each one. A single savings account works—just track the categories on a spreadsheet, in a notebook, or on a piece of paper taped to the fridge. Label the columns: category, monthly amount, total saved, amount needed, date due. Update it once a month during your check-in. It takes five minutes and it prevents you from accidentally spending your Christmas fund on a September impulse.

Some people prefer separate sub-accounts at an online bank—many of them let you create named "buckets" within a single account. If that works for how your brain organizes money, use it. The method matters less than the habit. The point is that when the expense arrives, the money is already sitting there, labeled, and waiting.

Most families need three to five sinking funds at any given time. Here's what a typical household set might look like.

**Car maintenance:** $50 a month. Covers oil changes, tire rotations, inspections, and builds a cushion for the repair you know is coming eventually.

**Medical:** $30 a month. Covers copays, prescriptions, the dental cleaning, the eye exam. Enough that a $200 bill doesn't send you scrambling.

**Holidays and birthdays:** $40 a month. Start in January. By November, you have $440 for gifts without touching a credit card. December stops being a financial emergency.

**Back-to-school or seasonal:** $25 a month starting after the holidays. By August, you've got $175 for clothes, supplies, and whatever fees the school sends home.

Total: $145 a month. That's not nothing—especially during a debt payoff. But it prevents $1,500 or more in charges that would otherwise go on a credit card throughout the year. Over time, sinking funds are one of the most effective tools for staying out of debt after you've paid it off.

A couple I know—we'll call them Deon and Tamara—started their sinking funds in month four of their reset. Tamara was skeptical. She said it felt like saving money they should be throwing at the debt. Every dollar sitting in a sinking fund was a dollar not attacking the balance. Deon agreed in theory, but he'd been the one scrambling every December to figure out how to buy gifts without the Visa. Two years in a row he'd put Christmas on the card and spent January hating himself for it. He was tired of the cycle.

They compromised: $100 a month total across three categories—holidays, car maintenance, and back-to-school. By December, they had $800 set aside for gifts. Tamara picked up a few things on Black Friday and paid cash. Deon ordered gifts online and used the debit card linked to the sinking fund. No card. No balance. No January guilt. It was the first holiday season in five years that didn't add to their debt. Tamara said that was the moment she stopped thinking of sinking funds as a luxury and started thinking of them as defense.

* * *

# Financial Habits That Prevent Backsliding

The emergency fund and sinking funds are the structural pieces. But protection also lives in the small daily habits your household builds during the reset. These are the behaviors that become automatic over time—the ones that keep you from drifting back into the patterns that created the debt in the first place.

Backsliding doesn't happen overnight. Nobody wakes up one morning and decides to undo six months of progress. It happens slowly. You skip a check-in because the week was crazy. Then you skip another one because nothing seemed urgent. A subscription reactivates and you don't catch it for three months. You stop checking the sinking fund balance because things feel stable. By the time you look up, the habits that were protecting you have gone quiet, and the old patterns have crept back in.

These five habits are the ones that prevent that drift. None of them take more than a few minutes. All of them pay for themselves many times over.

**Automate every bill.** Set up auto-pay for the minimum on every credit card and every recurring bill. Not because the minimum is your goal. Because a missed payment costs you $35 in fees, a potential rate increase, and a credit score hit. Auto-pay removes the risk of forgetting. You still make extra payments on top of it—but the floor is protected.

**Check your accounts weekly.** Not daily—that creates anxiety. Not monthly—that creates blind spots. Once a week, during your check-in, glance at every checking and savings balance. Look for charges you don't recognize. Look for subscriptions that reactivated. Look for patterns you didn't notice. Five minutes of weekly awareness prevents months of drift.

**Use a bill calendar.** Write down every bill and its due date on a monthly calendar—paper or digital, whatever you'll actually look at. Overlay your paydays. This shows you exactly which paycheck covers which bills and where the tight spots are. Most families discover that one pay period carries 70% of the bills while the other carries 30%. Seeing that pattern lets you plan instead of reacting.

**Review your credit card statements monthly.** Not just the balance. The charges. Fraud happens more often than people think. Small charges—$4.99, $9.99—can appear on your statement from services you never signed up for. Catching them early is free money. Missing them is a leak you already fixed once and shouldn't have to fix again.

**Keep the weekly check-in going.** Even after the debt is paid off. Especially after the debt is paid off. The check-in is the habit that holds all the other habits together. Without it, the rules fade, the sinking funds get raided, and the spending creeps back. Twenty minutes a week is a small price for financial peace.

None of these habits are exciting. That's the point. Protection isn't dramatic. It's boring, consistent, and effective. The families who stay out of debt after paying it off aren't doing anything extraordinary. They're doing ordinary things on a reliable schedule.

## Protect What You're Building

You're in Phase 3 of the 90-Day Family Debt Reset. By now, you've done more than most families ever do. You've faced the numbers. You've stopped the bleeding. You've chosen a payoff plan and started executing it. You've found hidden money, earned extra income, learned how to talk about it without fighting, built a set of rules, and prepared for setbacks.

This chapter is about making sure all of that work doesn't disappear the first time life tests you after the reset ends.

Because life will test you. The question isn't whether another big expense is coming. It's whether you'll have a thousand dollars sitting in a savings account when it does. Whether you'll have December's gifts already funded. Whether you'll catch the $9.99 charge from a service you never signed up for before it runs for six months.

The debt got you once. It doesn't get to do it again.

Monique told me something about a year after she finished her payoff. She said the strangest part wasn't being debt-free. It was how different emergencies felt. Before the reset, every unexpected expense came with a wave of dread —a tightness in her chest, a mental scramble to figure out which card still had room. After the reset, the same kinds of expenses still happened. But she'd check the emergency fund, transfer the money, and move on with her day. No panic. No card. No balance creeping back up.

She said, "The money part was actually the easy part. The hard part was believing I deserved to feel this calm about it."

You do. You're building toward it right now.

* * *

## This Week's Reset

**One.** Open a separate savings account for your starter emergency fund if you haven't already. Online banks take ten minutes to set up. Set an automatic transfer from checking—even $20 per paycheck—starting this week.

**Two.** Identify your top three sinking fund categories. Look at the calendar for the next six months. What predictable expenses are coming? Start setting aside a small amount each month, even if it's $10 per category to start.

**Three.** Set up auto-pay for the minimum on every credit card and recurring bill. Do it today. One missed payment costs more than the ten minutes this takes to set up.

**Four.** Build a bill calendar. Write down every due date and overlay your paydays. Identify which pay period is heavier and plan accordingly.

**Five.** Commit to continuing the weekly check-in beyond the 90-day reset. Put it on the calendar as a recurring event. The check-in is the habit that protects every other habit you've built.

You've been playing offense for two months. This chapter is about building the defense that makes sure you never have to start over. The emergency fund, the sinking funds, the automation, the habits—these are the walls around the progress you've made.

Next chapter is about something different. Something bigger than bills. We're going to talk about what your life looks like on the other side of this—and why that picture might matter more than any spreadsheet.



## CHAPTER 11

# Create Your Debt-Free Family Vision.

Carlos—the man with the sticky note on his bathroom mirror—told me something about seven months into his family's payoff. He said there was a Sunday afternoon when Janelle was in the kitchen and their daughter was on the floor drawing. He was sitting at the table with the laptop open, updating their debt snapshot, and the number had dropped below $10,000 for the first time. He stared at it for a while.

Then he closed the laptop, looked at his daughter, and thought: she's never going to know what this felt like.

Not the debt. The shame. The arguments at 11 PM. The way he used to check the mailbox with a knot in his stomach. The feeling of buying groceries and praying the card didn't decline in front of the cashier. The Sunday nights spent staring at a spreadsheet wondering if they'd ever get ahead of it. She would never carry that. Because he and Janelle were ending it. Right here. In this kitchen. With a spreadsheet and a pressure washer and a stubborn refusal to pass this down.

He didn't say any of this to Janelle. He just closed the laptop, sat on the floor next to his daughter, and watched her draw for a while. She was making a picture of their house with a big sun over it. He asked her if he could keep it. She said yes. He taped it next to the graph paper in his closet.

That's the moment this chapter is about. Not the mechanics. The meaning. The reason behind the grind that no spreadsheet can capture.

## Why Vision Fuels Discipline

For ten chapters, I've been asking you to do hard things. Face your numbers. Freeze your spending. Pick a payoff plan. Find hidden money. Earn more. Talk about it without fighting. Build rules. Survive setbacks. Protect what you've built. All of that takes discipline. And discipline runs on fuel.

The fuel isn't guilt. Guilt gets you through the first two weeks. After that, it turns into resentment—toward the budget, toward your partner, toward the whole process. Guilt is a starter, not a sustainer.

The fuel isn't fear either. Fear of another overdraft. Fear of the phone ringing. Fear of the balance going up. Fear works for a while, but living in fear month after month is exhausting. Eventually your brain stops responding to it because it can't sustain that level of anxiety forever.

The fuel that lasts is vision. A clear, specific, emotionally real picture of what your life looks like when the debt is gone. Not a vague hope. Not "it'll be nice." A picture with details in it. Details you can see when you're sitting at the kitchen table at 10 PM wondering if this is worth it.

It is worth it. But you need to know what the "it" is. Otherwise you're just running from something bad instead of running toward something good. And running from something only works until you're too tired to keep running.

$$* \quad * \quad *$$

## What Will Debt Freedom Make Possible?

I'm going to ask you a question, and I want you to actually answer it. Not skim past it. Not think about it abstractly. Write it down.

***What becomes possible for your family when you don't owe anyone anything?***

Sit with that for a minute. Because the answer is different for every household, and it's more specific than you think.

For some of you, debt freedom means saying yes to something you've been saying no to for years. The summer trip to see family you haven't visited since the kids were small. The birthday party your daughter wants that costs $300 and you'd be able to pay for without doing math in your head first. A weekend where money doesn't come up once. Just two days where nobody says "we can't afford that" or "maybe next month." Just normal. Just easy. That's all some of you want. And that's not a small thing.

For some of you, it's about leaving. Leaving the job you hate. Leaving the apartment that's too small. Leaving the city that costs too much. Debt pins you to your current situation because you can't afford the gap between here and there. Without it, the gap closes. Options open up that were invisible when every dollar had a creditor's name on it.

For some of you, it's about rest. Just… rest. Sleeping through the night without the 2 AM math running in your head. Checking the mail without your chest tightening. Opening the banking app because you want to, not because you're afraid of what you'll see. Sitting on the couch on a Friday night and not thinking about a single balance, a single payment, a single due date. The absence of financial anxiety is its own kind of freedom, and until you've felt it, you don't realize how heavy the weight has been. It's like carrying a backpack for so long that you forget it's there—until someone takes it off and your whole body feels different.

For some of you, it's about your kids. Saving for their future instead of paying off your past. Starting a college fund. Teaching them about money from a position of knowledge instead of shame. Showing them, by example, that debt is something you can get out of—not something you accept. Your daughter seeing you write the last check. Your son hearing you say "we're debt-free" and watching his face because he's old enough to know what that means.

And for some of you, it's about something you haven't let yourself think about yet. The house. The business. The retirement account that's been at zero. The giving you want to do. The life you stopped imagining because imagining it felt irresponsible when you still owed $19,000 on five credit cards.

That life isn't irresponsible. It's the reason you're doing all of this.

* * *

## Create Your Family Future List

This is the most personal exercise in the book. And for some of you, it will be the hardest—not because it requires math or spreadsheets, but because it requires you to believe that something better is coming.

Here's what I want you to do. Get a blank piece of paper. At the top, write: "When the debt is gone, our family will…"

Then finish that sentence as many times as you can. Don't filter. Don't edit. Don't worry about what's realistic. This isn't a budget. It's a vision. Write the things you want. The things you've stopped letting yourself want. The things you'd say to your partner at midnight if you weren't afraid of sounding naive.

Some of them will be big: buy a house, start a business, move to a new city. Some of them will be small: eat at a restaurant without checking the balance first, buy the kids name-brand shoes without doing the math, take a Saturday off without feeling guilty about not working a side job. Some of them will be about feeling something instead of having something: peace when the phone rings, pride when the bills are paid, the ability to say "yes" without hesitation for the first time in years. And some of them will surprise you. Things you didn't know you were carrying until you wrote them down. Dreams you buried so deep that it takes a quiet room and a blank page to find them again.

Do this together if you have a partner. Not during the check-in—this is separate. This is a conversation about dreams, not numbers. Pour some coffee. Sit on the couch. Let it be quiet. Let the list get long. Don't judge each other's items. If your partner wants a fishing boat and you want a spa day, both of those go on the list. This isn't about agreement. It's about honesty.

James and Tanya—from Chapter 7—wrote their list on a legal pad one evening after the kids went to bed. The house was quiet. Tanya started with practical things: pay off the car, build a real savings account, fix the bathroom that's been falling apart for two years. James was quiet for a while. He tapped the pen against the paper a few times. Then he wrote: take my mom on a trip before she can't travel anymore.

Tanya read it and didn't say anything for a minute. She told me later that it hit her differently than anything in the budget ever had. Because it wasn't about money. It was about time. And time was the thing the debt had been stealing from them all along. Then she added her own line: let the kids see us happy about money. Not stressed. Happy.

That list went on the refrigerator. Not the debt snapshot. Not the rules. The list. Because on the hard nights—the ones where the balance barely moved, or a setback hit, or they were just tired of saying no—that list reminded them why they were doing it. Not for the spreadsheet. For the mom. For the kids. For the bathroom. For the version of their life that was waiting on the other side.



## Replace Survival With Strategy

Most families in debt are in survival mode. You're not planning for the future. You're getting through the week. Every financial decision is reactive—something happens, you respond, you hope it works out. The grocery bill is higher than expected, so you skip the extra payment. The car needs gas and you're three days from payday, so the card comes out. There's no margin for thinking ahead because every dollar is already spoken for by the time it arrives.

Survival mode changes how you see yourself. You stop thinking of yourself as someone who builds wealth and start thinking of yourself as someone who manages crises. Your identity shrinks to fit the problem. And once that happens, the idea of dreaming—of wanting something more than just getting by—starts to feel reckless. Like you don't have the right to want a house when you still owe Discover $4,000.

You do have that right. And this chapter is about reclaiming it.

The 90-Day Family Debt Reset has been pulling you out of survival mode, chapter by chapter. You may not have noticed it happening because the changes were gradual. But look at where you are now compared to where you started.

You have a snapshot. You have a plan. You have rules. You have a safety net being built. You have a partner—or your own clarity—about how money works in your household. You're not reacting anymore. You're operating. There's a difference, and it's a bigger shift than the balance on any credit card.

The vision chapter is where that shift becomes permanent. Because once you've seen what your family's life could look like without debt, you can't unsee it. The list on the fridge isn't just motivation. It's a direction. It turns the payoff from a thing you're enduring into a thing you're building toward. And people who are building toward something make different decisions than people who are just trying to survive something.

You stop asking "can we afford this?" and start asking "does this move us closer to the list?" That filter changes everything. Not because the money is different. Because the thinking is.

* * *

## The Life You're Really Building

I want to be honest with you about something. Paying off credit card debt will not solve all your problems. It won't fix a broken marriage. It won't make a difficult job easier. It won't erase the years of stress you've already carried. Some things need time, therapy, rest, or conversations this book can't facilitate.

But I'll tell you what it does change. It removes the heaviest weight from the room.

When the debt is gone, arguments about money lose their edge. They might still happen—couples always have things to figure out—but they stop carrying the charge of $22,000 hanging over every word. When the debt is gone, decisions get lighter. You can think about what you want instead of what you owe. You walk through a store and the feeling is different. You're not calculating. You're just... shopping. When the debt is gone, the version of you that's been surviving starts to fade, and the version that's been waiting underneath it—the one who plans, who builds, who imagines—starts to show up again. Maybe slowly. Maybe in small ways at first. But you'll feel it.

That's who you're doing this for. Not the credit card company. Not your credit score. The person inside you who stopped dreaming because the bills wouldn't stop coming.

Andre is done with his debt now. All of it. He told me the night they made the last payment, Keisha ordered a pizza—the same thing they'd done when they paid off the first card. This time, Andre sat on the couch holding the receipt from the payment confirmation and didn't say anything for a while. Keisha asked if he was okay.

He said, "I'm trying to remember what I used to worry about before this. And I can't. That's how much space it was taking up."

Keisha laughed. Then she got quiet too. They sat there for a while, eating pizza, not talking about money for the first time in over a year. Not because they were avoiding it. Because there was nothing left to avoid.

That space is coming back to you. One payment at a time.

* * *

## This Week's Reset

**One.** Write your Family Future List. One piece of paper. "When the debt is gone, our family will…" Finish the sentence as many times as you can. Don't filter. Don't edit. Be honest about what you want.

**Two.** If you have a partner, do this together. Not during the check-in. A separate conversation. Somewhere quiet. Let the list get personal.

**Three.** Pick the three items on your list that matter most to your family right now. Circle them. These are your "why." When the process gets hard—and it will get hard again—these three things are the reason you keep going.

**Four.** Put the list somewhere you'll see it every day. The fridge. The bathroom mirror. The inside of the closet door where Carlos kept his graph paper. Let it live where the hard moments happen.

**Five.** Look at your current debt total. Then look at the list. The gap between those two numbers is closing. You're closer today than you were when you started this book. Let that be enough for tonight.

You've spent most of this book looking at what debt has taken from your family. This chapter asked you to look at what's waiting when it's gone. Hold onto that picture. It's the fuel that carries you through the months the spreadsheet can't.

One chapter left. Let's bring it all together.

## CHAPTER 12

# Your 90-Day Reset at a Glance.

You've done the work. You've read eleven chapters, faced hard truths, built systems, and made changes that most families never attempt. This chapter isn't new material. It's your playbook—everything you've learned, compressed into a reference you can come back to whenever you need to remember where you are, where you've been, and what to do next.

Dog-ear this chapter. Bookmark it. This is the one you return to on the hard nights when you need a reminder that the plan is still working, even when it doesn't feel like it.

* * *

## Month 1: Face It

Phase 1 is about honesty. You stop guessing, stop avoiding, and look at the full picture of your family's financial situation. This is the foundation everything else is built on.

### Chapter 1: How Your Family Got Here

Understand how ordinary life—not recklessness —creates credit card debt. Recognize the role of emergency spending, lifestyle creep, and the minimum payment trap. Release the shame. You're not broken. You need a reset.

**Chapter 2: Face It. Know Your Real Numbers.**

Build your Family Debt Snapshot: every card, every balance, every interest rate, every minimum payment, every due date. Calculate your total debt. Calculate your monthly income minus expenses. Stop guessing. Start knowing.

**Chapter 3: Freeze It. Stop the Bleeding.**

Define your household emergency rule. Remove credit cards from digital wallets and saved payment methods. Start your 30-day spending freeze. Set a small weekly cash allowance for each adult. If you still need the cards, track every charge and sort them into "had to" and "chose to."

***Month 1 Checklist***

☐ Debt Snapshot complete (all cards, balances, rates, minimums, due dates)

☐ Total debt calculated and written down

☐ Monthly income and expenses calculated

☐ Emergency rule defined and posted

☐ Credit cards removed from digital wallets and online accounts

☐ 30-day spending freeze started

☐ Weekly cash allowance set

☐ First weekly money check-in scheduled

* * *

# Month 2: Fix It

Phase 2 is about offense. You choose your attack plan, find hidden money, bring in extra income, and learn how to work through this with your partner without the conversation falling apart.

### Chapter 4: Fix It. Choose Your Debt Payoff Plan.

Learn the snowball method (smallest balance first), the avalanche method (highest interest rate first), and the hybrid method (quick win then switch to avalanche). Choose the one that fits your household. Circle your target card. Commit for 90 days before reconsidering. Start a tracking system—graph paper, spreadsheet, notebook—and record your starting total.

**Chapter 5: The Hidden $500.**

Run the Money Leak Audit: three months of statements, highlight every recurring charge, ask the three qualifying questions. Cancel every leak immediately. Address the silent budget killers: late fees, delivery markups, phone plan overpayment, insurance you haven't reviewed, food waste, bank fees. Call at least one credit card company to negotiate a lower rate. Check your state's unclaimed property website. Redirect every recovered dollar to your target card automatically.

**Chapter 6: Earn Your Way Out.**

Sell unused items from your house for fast income. Identify one service-based or skills-based side income source you can start this month. Avoid scams and MLMs. Set the rule: every dollar of side income goes to the target card the same week it's earned. Calculate your total monthly debt weapon—your Chapter 2 margin plus recovered leaks plus side income.

## Chapter 7: How to Talk About Debt Without Fighting.

Understand that debt is emotional before it's financial. Start the weekly money check-in: pick a day, start with a win, look at numbers together, plan the week ahead, end with agreement. Replace "you" with "we" when blame rises. If your partner won't engage, lower the stakes, share your fear first, and don't weaponize the book. Reset as a team: no scorecards, no secrets, shared sacrifice, celebrate wins out loud.

### *Month 2 Checklist*

- ☐ Payoff method chosen (snowball, avalanche, or hybrid)

- ☐ Target card identified and circled on debt snapshot

- ☐ Tracking system started (graph paper, spreadsheet, or notebook)

- ☐ Money Leak Audit completed

- ☐ All leaks canceled and recovered dollars redirected to target card

- ☐ At least one credit card rate negotiation attempted

- ☐ Unclaimed property search completed

□ At least 10 items listed for sale

□ One side income source identified and started

□ Every dollar rule in place for side income

□ Weekly money check-in running consistently

□ Total monthly debt weapon calculated

* * *

# Month 3: Future-Proof It

Phase 3 is about protection and vision. You build the systems that keep you from sliding backward and create a picture of the life you're fighting for.

**Chapter 8: Build Your Family Debt Rules.**

Write your Family Money Code: five to seven household rules in plain language. Include a spending threshold, a zero-balance rule for paid-off cards, a same-day transfer rule for extra income, and a commitment to the weekly check-in. Review the rules every week. Adjust as needed. Plan for predictable expenses with a monthly calendar look-ahead.

**Chapter 9: Handle Setbacks Without Giving Up.**

Write your bounce-back plan before you need it: under $500, $500–$2,000, over $2,000. When a hit lands: stop and assess, check your options, decide how to pay, adjust the plan but don't abandon it. After a bad month, name it at the check-in, diagnose the cause, and make the next month a recovery month. Never skip the check-in after a setback—that's the one that matters most.

## Chapter 10: Protect Your Finances From Future Damage.

Build a starter emergency fund: $1,000 target, automatic transfers, separate account. Start three to five sinking funds for predictable expenses: car maintenance, medical, holidays, back-to-school. Automate every bill. Use a bill calendar overlaid with paydays. Review credit card statements monthly for fraud and leaks. Keep the weekly check-in going permanently.

## Chapter 11: Create Your Debt-Free Family Vision.

Write your Family Future List: "When the debt is gone, our family will…" Circle the three items that matter most. Put the list somewhere visible. Let it fuel the discipline when guilt and fear run out. Replace survival thinking with strategic thinking. Remember what you're building toward.

### *Month 3 Checklist*

- ☐ Family Money Code written and posted
- ☐ Bounce-back plan written (three tiers)
- ☐ Starter emergency fund opened with automatic transfers
- ☐ At least two sinking fund categories started
- ☐ All bills on auto-pay
- ☐ Bill calendar created with paydays overlaid
- ☐ Family Future List written and posted
- ☐ Top three vision items circled
- ☐ Weekly check-in committed as a permanent household habit

* * *

# What Happens After Day 90

Day 91 is not the end. It's the beginning of the part where the system runs on its own.

By now, you have a debt snapshot you update monthly. A payoff method you're committed to. A leak audit you've completed and can re-run every quarter. Side income flowing. Weekly check-ins happening. A Money Code on the fridge. A bounce-back plan in the drawer. An emergency fund growing. Sinking funds absorbing predictable expenses. And a Family Future List reminding you why all of it matters.

That's not a 90-day program. That's a financial operating system for your household. The 90 days built it. Now you run it.

Here's what to focus on after day 90.

**Keep the check-in.** I cannot say this enough. The weekly check-in is the single habit that holds every other habit together. When couples stop checking in, the rules drift, the spending creeps, and the progress stalls. Twenty minutes a week. Protect it.

**Update your debt snapshot monthly.** Write the new total next to the old one. Watch the line go down. On bad months, the line flattens. On good months, it drops. Over time, the direction is unmistakable. That trend is your proof that the system works.

**Re-run the leak audit quarterly.**
Subscriptions reactivate. New charges appear.
Spending habits shift. Every three months, pull
the statements and check. Ten minutes can save
you $50 to $100 before it becomes a pattern.

**Grow the emergency fund.** Once you hit
$1,000, keep going. Add to it slowly. The
eventual target is one month of expenses, then
two, then three. You'll get there—probably
faster than you think, because the money that
used to go to credit cards will start going to
savings.

**When the last card hits zero, don't stop.** The
monthly payment you were making toward debt
doesn't become spending money. It becomes
savings, investment, sinking fund contributions,
or whatever your Family Future List says it
should be. The discipline you built didn't expire
when the balance did. Redirect it.

The families who stay debt-free aren't the ones
with the most money. They're the ones who kept
the system running after the urgency faded.
When the debt is gone and the pressure lifts,
the temptation is to relax everything. Let the

check-ins slide. Stop tracking. Start spending like the debt never happened. Don't. The system is what got you here. The system is what keeps you here.



## One Final Word

I started this book by telling you that you're not in debt because something is wrong with you. I want to end it the same way.

You picked up this book because you wanted something to change. And then you did the hardest thing a family can do with money: you looked at it honestly. You faced numbers most people spend years avoiding. You had conversations that scared you. You gave things up. You worked harder. You kept going after months that didn't go as planned.

That's not a person who's bad with money. That's a person who decided to fight for their family's future. And whether you're on day 30 or day 300, whether your balance is still high or almost gone, you're in a fundamentally different place than when you started. Not because the number changed. Because you did.

The 90-Day Family Debt Reset gave you a system. You gave it everything else—the courage, the honesty, the late nights, the hard conversations, the Saturdays you spent working instead of resting. The system is just a framework. You're the one who made it real.

Carlos took down the sticky note from his bathroom mirror the day the last card hit zero. He didn't throw it away. He folded it and put it in the same closet where the graph paper used to hang, next to his daughter's drawing of the house with the big sun.

He told me, "I want to remember what it felt like. Not the debt. The fight. Because that's the part I'm proud of."

You should be too.

# The Family Debt Reset Toolkit

These are the tools referenced throughout the book. Use them as-is, photocopy them, or download the printable versions at the link below.

Download printable versions: **aclpublishing.com/toolkit]**

Enter your name and email to get instant access to all nine worksheets as printable PDFs, plus bonus updates and resources as they become available.

* * *

## What's Inside

1. Debt Tracker

2. Credit Card Balance Sheet

3. Monthly Budget Template

4. Money Leak Audit

5. Family Money Meeting Guide

6. 90-Day Reset Checklist

# 1. Debt Tracker



List every credit card your household carries. Fill in each column. Update the balances monthly to track your progress.

| Card Name | Balance | APR % | Min. Payment | Due Date |
|---|---|---|---|---|
|  |  |  |  |  |
|  |  |  |  |  |
|  |  |  |  |  |
|  |  |  |  |  |
|  |  |  |  |  |
|  |  |  |  |  |
|  |  |  |  |  |

Total Credit Card Debt: $________________

Update this tracker on the first day of every month. Write each new total next to the previous one so you can see the trend.

# 2. Credit Card Balance Sheet

*Referenced in Chapter 4 — Use this to choose your payoff method.*

Sort your cards two ways. First by balance (smallest to largest) for the snowball method. Then by interest rate (highest to lowest) for the avalanche. Circle the card you're attacking first.

## Sorted by Balance (Snowball Order)

| Card Name | Balance | APR % | Min. Payment |
|---|---|---|---|
|  |  |  |  |
|  |  |  |  |
|  |  |  |  |
|  |  |  |  |
|  |  |  |  |

## Sorted by Interest Rate (Avalanche Order)

| Card Name | APR % | Balance | Min. Payment |
|---|---|---|---|

Payoff Method Chosen:  ☐ Snowball   ☐ Avalanche   ☐ Hybrid

Target Card: _______________

Monthly Extra Payment Amount: $_______________

# 3. Monthly Budget Template

*Referenced in Chapter 2 — Use this to see what comes in and what goes out.*

Fill in your actual numbers. Use net (after-tax) income. Pull spending amounts from your bank statements, not from memory.

## Income

| Source | Monthly Amount |
| --- | --- |
| Paycheck 1 (net) | $ |
| Paycheck 2 (net) | $ |
| Side Income (average) | $ |
| Other Income | $ |
| TOTAL INCOME | $ |

## Fixed Expenses

| Expense | Monthly Amount |
| --- | --- |
| Rent / Mortgage | $ |
| Car Payment | $ |
| Car Insurance | $ |
| Health Insurance | $ |
| Phone | $ |

| Internet | $ |
|---|---|
| Utilities (electric, gas, water) | $ |
| Childcare | $ |
| Student Loans | $ |
| Other Fixed | $ |
| TOTAL FIXED EXPENSES | $ |

## Variable Expenses

| Expense | Monthly Amount |
|---|---|
| Groceries | $ |
| Gas / Transportation | $ |
| Household Supplies | $ |
| Personal / Miscellaneous | $ |
| TOTAL VARIABLE EXPENSES | $ |

TOTAL INCOME:  $_____________

MINUS TOTAL FIXED:  $____________

MINUS TOTAL VARIABLE:  $_____________

= YOUR MONTHLY MARGIN:  $____________

This margin is the starting point for your extra debt payment. Add recovered leaks (Chapter 5) and side income (Chapter 6) to calculate your total monthly debt weapon.

# 4. Money Leak Audit

*Referenced in Chapter 5 — Use this to find the money you're already losing.*

Pull three months of bank and credit card statements. Highlight every recurring charge. For each one, answer the three questions below. If all three answers are NO, it's a leak. Cancel it immediately.

## The Three Questions

1. Did I use this in the last 30 days?

2. If I canceled today, would it affect my household this week?

3. Would I sign up for this again right now at this price?

| Charge / Service | Monthly $ | Used? | Need? | Re-sign? |
| --- | --- | --- | --- | --- |
|  |  |  |  |  |
|  |  |  |  |  |
|  |  |  |  |  |
|  |  |  |  |  |

Total Monthly Leaks Found:  $_______________
Date All Leaks Canceled:  _______________

## Silent Budget Killers Checklist

☐ Late fees eliminated (auto-pay set on all cards)

☐ Delivery/convenience fees reduced or eliminated

☐ Car insurance reviewed and compared

☐ Phone plan reviewed and switched if savings available

☐ Food waste reduced (meal planning started)

☐ Bank fees reviewed (overdraft, maintenance, ATM)

☐ Credit card rate negotiation attempted

☐ Unclaimed property search completed

# 5. Family Money Meeting Guide

*Referenced in Chapter 7 — Use this to run your weekly check-in.*

Pick the same day and time every week. Keep it to 20 minutes. Follow this agenda.

## Weekly Check-In Agenda

1. Start with a win. Each person shares one thing that went well with money this week.

2. Review the numbers. Pull up balances. What came in? What went out? Any surprises?

3. Review the rules. Did we follow the Family Money Code this week? Any adjustments needed?

4. Look ahead. Any big expenses coming next week? Birthdays, bills, car stuff?

5. Agree on one thing. One action or adjustment you'll both commit to for the coming week.

## Ground Rules for the Check-In

- ☐ No blame. Replace "you" with "we."

- ☐ No surprises. Both partners see the same numbers.

☐  No lectures. End with agreement, not assignment.

☐  If tension rises, pause. Come back to it in 24 hours.

☐  The check-in after a bad month is the most important one. Never skip it.

Our check-in day and time: _______________

# 6. 90-Day Reset Checklist

*Referenced in Chapter 12 — Use this to track your progress through each phase.*

## Phase 1: Face It (Month 1)

- ☐ Debt Snapshot complete
- ☐ Total debt calculated and written down
- ☐ Monthly income and expenses calculated
- ☐ Emergency rule defined and posted
- ☐ Credit cards removed from digital wallets
- ☐ 30-day spending freeze started
- ☐ Weekly cash allowance set
- ☐ First weekly check-in scheduled

## Phase 2: Fix It (Month 2)

- ☐ Payoff method chosen (snowball / avalanche / hybrid)
- ☐ Target card identified and circled
- ☐ Tracking system started
- ☐ Money Leak Audit completed
- ☐ All leaks canceled
- ☐ Credit card rate negotiation attempted

☐ At least 10 items listed for sale

☐ One side income source started

☐ Every-dollar rule in place for side income

☐ Weekly check-in running consistently

☐ Total monthly debt weapon calculated

## Phase 3: Future-Proof It (Month 3)

☐ Family Money Code written and posted

☐ Bounce-back plan written (3 tiers)

☐ Emergency fund opened with auto-transfer

☐ At least 2 sinking fund categories started

☐ All bills on auto-pay

☐ Bill calendar created

☐ Family Future List written and posted

☐ Top 3 vision items circled

☐ Weekly check-in committed as permanent habit

# 7. Emergency Spending Rules

*Referenced in Chapter 3 — Define what counts as a real emergency before one happens.*

Write your household's emergency definition below. Post it on the fridge or in the kitchen drawer next to the credit card. When a spending moment comes, check the list before reaching for the card.

## The Three-Question Test

Before using the credit card, ask:

1. Is someone's health or safety at risk?

2. Can this wait 48 hours?

3. Can we cover it with what's in checking or the emergency fund?

If the answers are NO, YES, or YES — the card stays in the drawer.

## YES, It's an Emergency

# NO, It's Not an Emergency

Both partners must agree on this list. Review it monthly during your check-in.

# 8. Side Income Brainstorm Sheet

*Referenced in Chapter 6 — Use this to identify your fastest path to extra income.*

## Fast Income (This Week)

Items in your house you can sell right now:

1.
2.
3.
4.
5.
6.
7.
8.
9.
10.

Platform(s) to list on: _______________
Estimated total from sales:  $_______________

## Service-Based Income (This Month)

Services you could offer in your neighborhood:

1.
2.
3.

How to advertise: _______________

Estimated income per job: $_______________


## Skills-Based Income (Ongoing)

Skills you have that people pay for:

1.

2.

3.


Platform to start on: _______________

Estimated monthly income (conservative): $_______________


## Your Total Monthly Debt Weapon

Chapter 2 margin:  $_______________

Chapter 5 recovered leaks:  $_______________

Side income (estimated):  $_______________

TOTAL:  $_______________


Rule: Every dollar of side income goes to the target card the same week it's earned.

# 9. Debt-Free Vision Worksheet

*Referenced in Chapter 11 — This is the most personal page in the book.*

Complete the sentence below as many times as you can. Don't filter. Don't edit. Be honest about what you want.

## When the debt is gone, our family will...

## Our Top 3 (Circle These)

From the list above, pick the three that matter most to your family right now. Circle them. These are your "why."

1.

2.

3.

Put this page somewhere you'll see it every day. The fridge. The bathroom mirror. The closet door. Let it remind you what you're fighting for on the nights when the spreadsheet can't.

* * *

Download all nine worksheets as printable PDFs at:

**aclpublishing.com/toolkit**

Enter your name and email for instant access, plus updates and bonus resources.

**About the Author**

Anthony C. Lumpkin is an entrepreneur, author, and founder of ACL Publishing. He has spent over fifteen years building businesses and helping families navigate real-world financial challenges. He wrote The Family Debt Reset because he believes working households deserve a debt plan that respects their intelligence, addresses their relationships, and fits the way they actually live. He lives in Ohio with his wife Micole. This is one of several titles in the ACL Publishing catalog. For free tools and resources, www.aclpublishing.com